Yat Wit

Yat Wit

Chicken Gumbo for the New Orleans Soul

Yvonne Spear Perret

PELICAN PUBLISHING COMPANY

GRETNA 2011

The word "Pelican" and the depiction of a pelican are trademarks of Pelican Publishing Company, Inc., and are registered in the U.S. Patent and Trademark Office.

Library of Congress Cataloging-in-Publication Data

Perret, Yvonne Spear.
  Yat wit : chicken gumbo for the New Orleans soul / Yvonne Spear Perret.
      p. cm.
  ISBN 978-1-58980-907-9 (pbk. : alk. paper)   1.   New Orleans (La.)—Social life and customs. 2.   New Orleans (La.)—Humor. I. Title.
  F379.N55P47 2011
  976.3'35—dc22

                                        2011002664

Printed in the United States of America
Published by Pelican Publishing Company, Inc.
1000 Burmaster Street, Gretna, Louisiana 70053

To Vincent and Valjean,
from whence this Yat *and her* Wit *originated*
and
to my hometown, New Orleans

Contents

Definition

Yat \ yăt \ n. : Originally, a term used to denote a resident from one of several New Orleans neighborhoods whose phraseology and pronunciation are distinctive. Now often used as a generic term for "New Orleanian."

The word "yat" is a derivation of the common greeting "Where y'at?"

Literally translated to the equally ungrammatical "Where are you at?", the phrase actually means "Hi. How are you?"

I didn't even know I was a *yat* until I started college at an uptown university. Though my official status was "Town Student," my new friends who hailed from around the country proudly introduced me to others as a "yat," and I was pleased to wear the label.

Though some locals may still consider the term to have a negative connotation because of the less-than-upper-class neighborhoods from which it originated, I certainly never felt it a put-down.

Since Hurricane Katrina, I consider it a term of endearment.

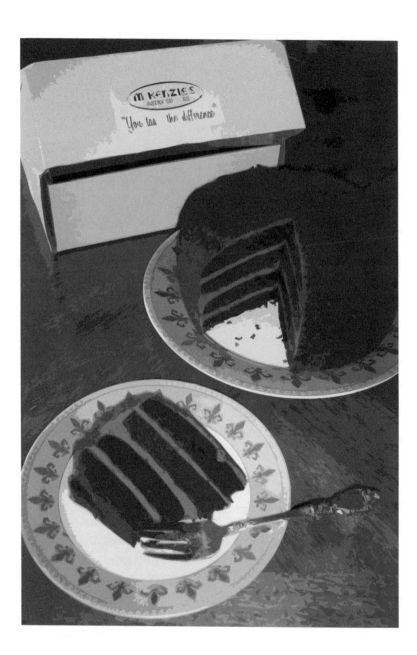

Introduction

It took a village to raise this yat—a village that started, of course, with my "mom 'n'em." Mom, a science teacher, is a buoyantly cheerful Cajun who skillfully raised eight children. "'N'em" includes a razor-sharp-witted, rocket-scientist dad; treasured aunts like Tante, Tee-tant, and Titine; godparents Na-nan and Pa-ran; four uniquely quirky grandparents; seven unnecessary siblings; and dozens of reprobate cousins to lead me into temptation.

But the village extended even further. For better or worse, my development—arrested or otherwise—was influenced by some of the most beloved and/or questionable of New Orleans characters.

We'll start with Miss Linda, of "Romper Room" fame, who convinced me at a very young age that it was better to be a well-behaved little *Do-Bee, not* a miscreant *Don't-Bee.* And although this lesson should have remained my lifelong guiding principle, I must confess I've had my fair share of *Don't-Bee* moments, and—boy—were they the fun ones!

Of course, the nuns who ruled the classrooms and hallways of St. Frances Cabrini School in Gentilly would have none of this nonsense known as fun, and the good Sisters had slightly-short-of-torture remedies to get me back on track.

Even worse, when Christmas rolled around, regrets over

Don't-Bee moments came back to haunt me big time. I had to worry not only about what Santa had seen during the year but also about what Mr. Bingle might know about my past.

Thank goodness I had Uncle Henry and the Great McNutt to lighten the mood. Then again, Morgus and Chopsley were always good for a laugh and a scare.

My teen years were influenced by people like John Pela, who made me think I could dance, and the DJs at 'TIX and 'RNO, who spun the tunes to foster this delusion. Meanwhile, Dick Bruce launched my lifelong addiction to McKenzie's doughnuts, that is, until McKenzie's closed and I required intervention therapy. The Saints taught me to hold on to my dreams, for one day those dreams might come true in a super way. On the other hand, Chris Owens gave me hopes of blossoming into voluptuous curves one day (uh, didn't happen).

Surrounded by these characters—and countless quirky others—it's a wonder any of us yats turn out to be normal. But then what fun is there in being normal anyway? If I were normal, I wouldn't scream, "Hey, Mister!" at the top of my lungs to a man I've never met, hoping to get a trinket that I already have two dozen of. I wouldn't drive across town in a futile search for the latest version of a blackout cake that someone said tastes just like McKenzie's, knowing full well that it couldn't possibly. I wouldn't have visions of Sr. Clare Agnes pop into my head and make me do the right thing when for one split second I consider keeping the extra dollar the cashier at Rouses mistakenly hands me. I wouldn't whoop for joy when the Tulane Green Wave scores a touchdown, hoping against hope that one day their future might hold a fate as improbable as the Saints'.

But in the end, I think the greatest influence on me was the city herself. New Orleans is a lot like that one zany aunt found in just about every local family. You know, the one who's a little too raucous at times; the one who's not embarrassed to laugh out loud, often at herself; the one who's always ready to scoop you up in a warm, breasty hug whenever you come to visit. She's suffered staggering tragedies during her lifetime, but her spirit is indomitable and her countenance carefree.

Sure, she's got a few too many wrinkles. And, yes, she wears too much makeup. And, lord, does she dress inappropriately! But everyone who knows her adores her.

A party just isn't a party without her.

And when I grow up, I want to be just . . . like . . . her!

Yat Wit

Beignet Gris-Gris

At first glance they don't *look* controversial. To the contrary, it is precisely their gastronomic simplicity that has kept them so popular for so long. No delicate pastry here. No gourmet custard inside. No fancy fondant on top. Just hearty, unpretentious lumps of fried bread dough doused in sugar.

Served in orders of three.

And therein lies the first controversy.

Why three?

The numbers just don't add up. The natural pattern most people adopt while enjoying an order of café au lait and beignets is as follows: sip of coffee, bite of beignet, sip of coffee, bite of beignet, etc. This instinctive regimen requires one cup of coffee and *exactly two* beignets for everything to work out perfectly in the end. Two, not three. The person who follows the sip/bite pattern will have one sip of coffee remaining, just enough to wash down that last bite of the second beignet.

That leaves one beignet untouched on the plate and a customer who is sufficiently full. At this point, the patron must use incredible willpower to resist that third doughnut or—like 99 percent of the rest of us—give in and stuff it down. Even Jimmy Buffett lamented the problem:

Coffee is strong at the Café Du Monde.
Donuts are too hot to touch.
Just like a fool, when those sweet goodies cool
I eat 'til I eat way too much.
      —from "The Wino and I Know"

The number game gets even worse when there are two people at the table, especially young lovers on an awkward first date. If they walked in looking for an agreeable way to end the evening, they're in for a big disappointment—or worse. Beignet gris-gris begins its mischief as soon as they sit down.

Not wanting to appear piggish, they each deny that they could possibly down three doughnuts on their own, so the couple agrees to split an order. But do the math. Three beignets are not evenly divisible by two people. So, after each person has had one doughnut, the trouble begins. With half a cup of coffee remaining, the couple makes polite conversation, all the while casting surreptitious glances at that third little gem lying buried in powdered sugar on the plate. He wants it, but being the chivalrous gentleman that he is, he insists she take it. She wants it, but being the demure young lady that she is, she resists and offers it to him.

Yes, they both covet it mightily, but neither is willing to indulge, knowing that while he or she is enjoying that last beignet, the other person can only watch and pretend to be satisfied with the now-cold, few sips of coffee left in the cup. Or worse yet, convinced that the other person really doesn't want it, they both reach for it at the same time. Uh-oh. Awwwk-ward!

As a result, many a third beignet—though fiercely desired— has gone uneaten, untouched, forsaken on the plate. The discontented couple leaves the table unsatisfied, and what could have been a promising relationship is now in jeopardy.

So, if two beignets is the perfect number, why are there three beignets to an order? For the answer to this question, you'll have to go back in time about a century and half and look for the greedy, market-savvy vendor who came up with this slick selling tactic after concluding that, although two beignets provide the ideal accompaniment for a cup of coffee, he could charge more for three doughnuts and thus make more money. I hope he earns another day in purgatory for every relationship he has doomed over the years.

Unfortunately, the beignet curse doesn't end with the math dilemma. Consider physics. What engineering genius came up with the idea of putting powdered sugar in a metal shaker that has teeny, tiny little holes in the top? A metal shaker that sits in oppressively damp New Orleans humidity for days on end.

Okay, position this can directly over your beignets, turn the can upside down, and give it a gentle shake.

Do you *really* expect individual little grains of sugar— each hardly heavy enough to be subject to gravity at all—to find their way through those tiny little holes in the top of the can? The same tiny holes that are caked closed by the humidity? It doesn't take a Michoud scientist to know that it's just not going to happen.

Don't look now, but your beignets are still naked.

You could try hitting the can on the table to partially clear the holes, then turning the shaker upside down over the beignets and rapping with your knuckles on the bottom of the can with brute force. If you're not one to be embarrassed by the racket you're making, sugar will indeed fall, albeit reluctantly, to the top of the beignets.

Yet the noise could be the least of your worries. Leave it to beignet gris-gris to reveal the darker side of humanity. Due to a misplaced trust in human nature, I once turned the shaker upside down to start shaking and rapping—unaware that the immature jokester who previously sat at my table had unscrewed the lid of the metal can before leaving. Unfortunately, this is a common prank, especially among the teenage set, and unfortunately, I learned it the hard way—sitting there in a dark business suit and in the company of visiting business colleagues whom I was trying hard to impress. Yes, you could say I made an impression.

Patrons shouldn't even count on being able to breathe normally when around beignets. Inhale while taking a bite, and powdered sugar rushes into the lungs resulting in an embarrassing episode of "Confectioner's Cough." Exhale while taking a bite, and—like confetti in front of a fan—a shower of sugar fills the air.

Never, ever laugh when holding a beignet.

And leave it to beignets to bring out the worst in people's table manners. Ever shared a table with a dunker? While some are sufficiently well mannered, far too many make it a practice to plunge the entire beignet into the cup of coffee, let it soak, and then bring it to their mouths, dripping hot coffee and soggy dough along the way. This delightful show is often accompanied by loud slurping noises. Equally appetite suppressing is the slob who tears the beignet into little pieces, tosses them into the cup of coffee, and then fishes them out with his fingers. Also often accompanied by loud slurping noises.

So is there no bright side to beignets? Well, in the "good news" department, a friend once told me that beignets were not as fattening as one might think because of the large pockets of air often found in the middle of the doughnuts. And indeed, I have used this fact to soothe my conscience when I'm finishing off that third, unnecessary beignet. What my friend's cheery rose-colored glasses fail to see, however, is the other side of the air-pocket story. The "air" in that air pocket is actually superheated steam waiting to sear the entire interior of your mouth, making every subsequent bite tasteless, not to mention excruciatingly painful. So much for the bright side.

Ah, beignets.

Three simple lumps of fried bread dough doused in sugar— and poised for peril.

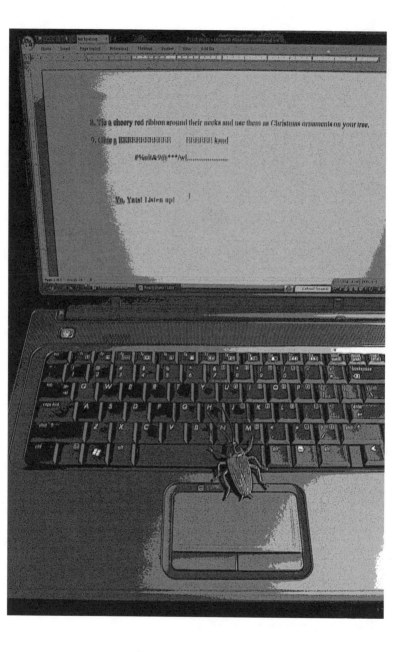

8. Tie a cheery red ribbon around their necks and use them as Christmas ornaments on your tree.

9. Glue a RRRRRRRRRRRRR   RRRRRR kind

#%u&&9@***/wt.....................

. Yo, Yuis! Listen up!

Roach, Interrupted

The only good roach is a dead roach. They are filthy, vile, disgusting creatures who slithered into existence only by a freak foul-up of the Creator in His exhaustion on the sixth day.

Scientists say their species will outlast ours. So the ideal goal—total eradication of *blattaria dictyoptera*—may not be realistic. The best we can hope for, then, is to kill as many as we can. Even that solution leaves us with a messy clean-up issue: what to do with all the carcasses? Not to worry. Consider the following:

1. Spray a few roach carcasses with gold paint, glue safety pins to their tummies, and give Mignon Faget a run for her money.

2. Use them as biodegradable packing material instead of landfill-clogging Styrofoam peanuts. It's the environmentally responsible solution.

3. Choose one as your game piece when you're playing Monopoly to indicate your intent to become the slumlord for all the cheap properties.

4. Use a roach cadaver to plug up the hole in your screen so the mosquitoes can't get in.

5. Put silver hoops through a matching pair of them and wear them as earrings on Halloween.

6. Tie a string to one of them and pull it around the house to give your fat, lazy cat some exercise.

7. Put one on the pillow in your guest bedroom for visitors who have overstayed their welcome.

8. Tie a cheery red ribbon around their necks and use them as Christmas ornaments on your tree.

9. Glue a EEEEEEEEEEEE EEEEEE ksnd
    #%uit&9@***/wl......................

Yo, yats! Listen up.

I had to chase the broad out of the room. I mean, like, I been clinging to the wall behind her, twitching my little antennas, watching her type this tripe, and biding my time. Well, enough is enough.

So, I put my shiny black wings into first gear and took off. A double loop around the lamp, a whiz past her left ear, then a dive-bomb run right into the middle of her computer screen. I wish you could've heard the sucker scream. She shot out of this room like a dingbat outta hell. And she won't be back tonight, believe me. This computer could crash and burn, but you can bet your can of Raid that she won't come back in here. Man, it was so easy; I'm almost ashamed of myself. Almost.

So now it's my turn at the keyboard. My name is Vincent. Here's my card:

Vincent

Flying Cockroach Extraordinaire

Homes   **Boats**   **Cars**
Commercial and Residential
Late Night Appointments a Specialty

Now that we know each other real good, let's get to it.

Us roaches have gotten a bum rap in this town ever since you two-legged wimps paddled up the bayous and invaded our turf. And in all that time, you've been trying to get rid of us. *Total eradication,* the broad said. Well, here's a newsflash: we ain't goin' nowhere. For every one of us you manage to assassinate, there's thousands more to carry on. So, forget the yummy poison tablets you throw under your sink. Forget the friendly pest-control man with the big, mean spray gun. (Ooh, like I'm really scared!) And forget the sweet little roach hotels you put in your bedroom closets. Why would we settle for one of the cheap plastic hotels when we've already got deluxe accommodations in every swanky joint in the metro area?

And hey! Before you call us *filthy* and *vile,* take a look in the mirror, cap. We roaches have seen the seamy side of human workings. You talk about wanting to be a fly on the wall? Well, I been a roach on the wall. I've heard enough wheeling and dealing to send a busload of officials up the river. And I've hidden in the plush carpet of boardrooms where deals were cut that would make J. R. Ewing squirm.

So, clean up your act first and then maybe we'll clean up ours.

In the meantime, permit me to brag about some of the talents we have honed and perfected over the millennia.

Ambush is a specialty. The beauty of this tactic lies in its simplicity. We just gotta pick a good place—like next to the switch on a lamp. Then, when you reach under the lampshade to turn on the light . . . surprise!

Another primo spot is behind the shampoo bottle on the bathtub rim. We've learned to wait till the victim is dripping wet and has a face full of soap. Then we spring. It's amazing how fast all sense of modesty dies when a close encounter of the roachy kind sends a shrieking naked human bolting from the bathroom.

My cousin Vern deserves special mention in the ambush category. He patiently hid inside a shower cap until a doe-eyed college coed donned it and tucked in all her long tresses. The next thing she hears is the pitter patter of little roach feet scrambling around inside the cap, and it sends her shrieking au naturel into the hallway. Priceless!

And hey, did you hear about that dude in Mandeville who went to use his barbecue pit for the first time last summer without having cleaned it at the end of the previous season? It literally exploded with roaches when he opened it. A surging, undulating mass of roaches blanketed the ground where he stood, and hundreds of us made it up his pants legs before he could make a getaway. Gives a whole new meaning to the phrase "fire up the grill!"

Ambush is indeed fun, but nothing beats direct assault. So, let's ratchet things up a bit—as we take flight! Yes, sirree, for pure fear factor, nothing can top a huge brown bug with shiny, black, beating wings coming straight at you in the middle of the night. Guaranteed to rattle the stalwart and terrify the weak-hearted.

The most accomplished pilots can make pinpoint landings on some particularly effective places of the human anatomy. The first is in the middle of the back—you know that one spot that you can't reach to scratch when it itches. Barbecues and parties held outside at night provide ideal working conditions. The victim might not even know one of us has made a precise landing on this prized target area. Before long, though, someone else discovers the fact. The discoverer immediately commences pointing and stuttering and stuttering and pointing. This causes the victim to run around in circles while trying to reach the unreachable spot. If the victim is female, she is probably screaming hysterically by this point. If he is male, he is probably trying to act real cool about it, but believe me, he is freaked. Chances are, he looks like he's having a seizure as he tries to bat and swipe at his own back while "nonchalantly" turning in circles. Heaven forbid that a friend would swat it off for him, lest the roach turn on him next. Meanwhile, the courageous roach just clamps his hairy little legs onto the shirt, knowing he is safely out of range. Gawd, I love it!

Now, before we chat about the absolute best place to land on the human body, allow me to properly set the scene. It's the middle of the night. The targeted party is deep asleep, preferably dreaming. Then all of a sudden—whoosh! A dive-bombing cockroach flies from the top of the wall right onto the victim's face. Eyeballs spring open to see magnified, close-up views of hairy little roach legs and twitching antennas. Talk about a nightmare! But—hee, hee—it's real, sucka! The roach scrambles around on the person's face during the couple of seconds before the rest of the victim's fear-paralyzed muscles can get moving, and then the roach makes its getaway. It takes precise timing and it's risky, but it's worth it, because now there's one more human who will never sleep soundly again for the rest of his life. Huzzah!

Alas, all good things must come to an end, but not before executing one final feat. One of the rewards of being a roach is knowing that after a lifetime of bugging humans (excuse the pun), we also get the last laugh after we die. Elephants aren't the only creatures who go to a special place to die. So do us roaches. Though sick, mutilated, and dying, every brother roach uses his last ounce of strength to make it to a meaningful resting place—such as deep inside a shoe. Then he can die in peace, knowing that one day some poor sucker will slip his or her (hopefully barefoot) toesies deep down into that shoe and find the crunchy corpse lying in wait there.

Or how about a drinking glass? An opaque and tall one, if at all possible. It's gross enough to see the carcass floating in the glass when you fill it with milk first thing in the morning, but kudos to the roaches who aren't discovered until the unsuspecting human has taken his first swig. Bottoms up!

Well, enough bragging.

That poor broad who owns this computer is probably asleep by now. Deep asleep. The sheets have probably fallen away from her face. So, looks like I got a job to do. Know what I mean?

Later, y'all.

The Thrill of the Grab

It's Mardi Gras.

High above the crowd, a float rider dangles the prize. It is a plastic necklace, a really long one, and it has the krewe's insignia medallion. You want those beads.

In a gesture meant to taunt and tease, the rider twirls the beads around one finger, then gathers them back up into his hand. To him this is all just a game, but to you this is serious business. You *have* to have those beads.

When he finally tires of taunting the waiting crowd, he winds up and prepares to throw. Suddenly, everything switches to slow motion. His fingers slowly uncurl from the necklace as it sails out of his grasp, headed in your direction. It does a graceful, perfectly executed pirouette in midair. Each individual plastic bead catches the rays of the sun, creating a prism of sparkling beauty.

You know more than ever that this necklace was meant for you.

Your hand reaches up. The beads have reached the apex of their ascent into the air and then begin to fall toward the earth, toward you. Your heart beats a little quicker in anticipation. Soon, the prize will be in your hands. Then you sense the presence of other hands around you, all mistakenly convinced that the beads were meant for them.

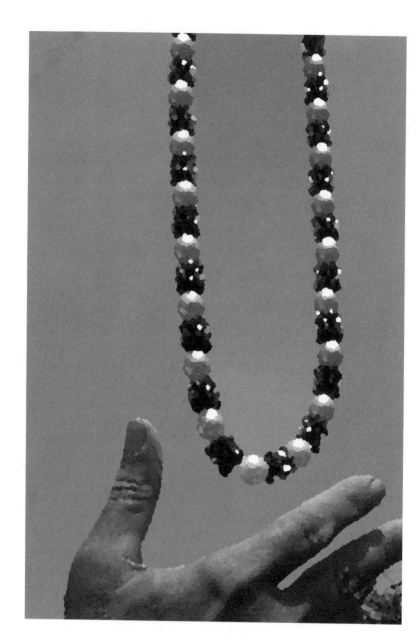

The adrenaline courses through your veins, preparing you to triumph over all other competitors.

You bend your knees, never taking your eyes from the jewels you were destined to possess. Then, with precision timing, you spring into the air as your hand stretches high, high, higher, above the madding crowd. Finally, the necklace hits your hand, and your fingers curl tightly around the prize. The beads are yours—yours alone! Intense gratification and pleasure sweep through your body. You are experiencing . . .

"The Thrill of the Grab"!

The titillating sensation you feel upon this victory is no less exhilarating than what you would feel if you had made a diving catch in centerfield to win the World Series; no less exciting than what you would feel if you had caught a Hail Mary pass to lead the Saints to another Super Bowl victory.

As your feet reach the ground again, you smile in triumph and admire the intrinsic beauty of the plastic beads you have caught. Then . . .

. . . you toss them into a sagging grocery bag with the other fifty-eight conquests you made that day, including five other beads exactly like the ones you just snatched. And there in that grocery bag those beads are destined to remain, stored away in the attic for years, or until your brother-in-law needs them for a truck parade.

A marching band passes by and you pretend to care. But the next float is coming your way. You have already spotted the third rider on the top deck; he is holding a long string of pearls. The float draws nearer. The rider gathers the strand of beads up into his hand and winds up for the pitch. You catch his eye for just a moment, and suddenly you know for a fact that those pearls are meant for you. . . .

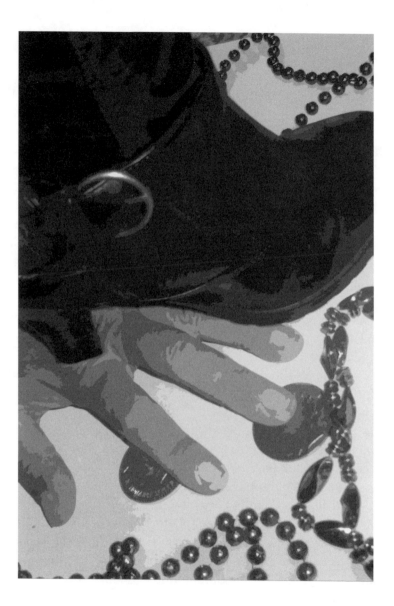

A Guide for Mardi Gras Virgins

If you're a seasoned pro, you can skip this chapter.

However, if you're a tourist, a first-timer, or just want to catch more stuff than the uninformed masses, read on. . . .

In the previous chapter you became familiar with the Thrill of the Grab—an inspiring, satisfying experience if ever there was one. But in real life along a parade route, things may not always go so smoothly. For example, what happens if at the precise moment you are experiencing the Thrill of the Grab, the person next to you is doing the same—and with the same beads that you have a hold on?

A gentle tug on the beads will usually reveal who has the better hold on the prize, indicating the individual who was predestined by the Mardi Gras fates to have the beads in the first place. If this does not decide the winner, you and your competitor will probably face each other with an embarrassed smile, which suggests that the fleeting Thrill of the Grab has already passed and you've both realized you're fighting over a plastic trinket worth two cents. Then one of you will let go—usually the more intelligent of the two.

In certain other instances, there is universal agreement on the following:

⚜ Tie goes to the tourist. It's good PR for the city, and

besides, the tourist has spent a hell of a lot more money than the native to get to this parade. Let him feel as if he got something for his money.

✤ Tie goes to the kid. Any adult who would fight with a child over Carnival beads is a Mardi Gras Scrooge. (Exception: If the article being fought over is not beads but rather a pair of thong bikinis, this rule does not apply.)

✤ Tie goes to the lady. The beads will look better on her anyway, and the friendly gesture makes a guy appear generous ("generous" being a relative term, seeing that as gifts go, necklaces just don't come any cheaper than "free").

Doubloons

Because they're more difficult to catch, doubloons pose a special problem. An "air grab" can be tough, but if you can manage it, the thrill involved is worth the trouble.

On the other hand, if you're looking to go home with lots of doubloons, the best strategy is to forego the airborne thrill and instead hit the ground as soon as the rider lets go with a fistful. Statistics support this strategy; 78 percent of all doubloons are retrieved off the ground rather than caught in midair. Of course, there's not much thrill in a "ground grab," but there's significant satisfaction in showing the guy next to you the three doubloons you scrounged off the ground after he tried for the more macho "air grab"—and came up with nothing.

Important note for Mardi Gras virgins: if you've decided to go for the "ground grab," place your foot—not your hand—over a rolling doubloon. This is accepted as legal claim. Then you can lift your foot and pick up the doubloon. If you use your fingers first instead of your foot, your hand is at the mercy of seasoned Carnival-goers who automatically stomp down on grounded doubloons. And if that stomping foot is encased in a cowboy boot or stiletto heel, you can forget retrieving any other doubloons or beads for the rest of the Carnival season.

Cups

The most utilitarian of all throws (you can actually use them in real life), cups are also the most difficult of throws to catch. In fact, more than any other throw, catching cups is often a matter of luck.

A sudden shift in wind direction will change their trajectory when they're just inches from your reach. And because of a cup's shape, one-handed catches are pretty difficult. A tossed cup will bounce from hand to hand to hand in the crowd before someone finally gets the right grip on it. So, just as with doubloons, a "ground grab" might be your best bet.

In General

If you want to catch lots of stuff, be one of the following:

⚜ Tall.

⚜ A sweet old lady sitting on a folding chair in the back row.

⚜ Good-looking, well proportioned, and young—and not afraid to flaunt it.

⚜ If you are none of the above, you can increase your chances by borrowing an adorable child from a relative or neighbor. Cute kids are Mardi Gras magnets. Have the little darling sit on top of your ladder while you stand behind her, beaming proudly as if she were your very own. You'll be pelted with stuff to bring home—if you can pry it from the little brat's fingers.

If you are a Carnival neophyte, you may feel at a disadvantage because this is your first time. But you have something that the others around you do not. You, my friend, have the opportunity to experience the exhilarating ecstasy of "the first time"; to savor the singularly stimulating excitement that comes once and only once; to undergo a transforming, thrilling, once-in-a-lifetime experience. Enjoy every moment, then bask in the honey-sweet afterglow.

For although there may be many wonderful parades in your future—parades that you will thoroughly enjoy—you may often find yourself reminiscing about this very first one and sighing out loud, like countless others before you: *"Ah, to be a Mardi Gras virgin again!"*

Spell Check

There's something innately insulting about having one's language skills questioned and held suspect by a machine. Anyone who's entered text into a Word document has encountered them: the built-in reprimands announcing that one has committed either a greevous spelling errer (red wavy underline) or an even worser grammatical error (green wavy underline).

After having the rules of grammar pounded into my head throughout elementary school by the good Sisters of St. Joseph, I take any such admonition by my computer as a personal insult to both me and Sr. Mary Phillip.

However, just try to type anything about New Orleans, and the red and green wavy lines light up like a Christmas tree. Many of our most respectable words and phrases are maliciously maligned. They are unfairly judged to be nonexistent, incorrectly used, or inaccurately spelled.

Mardi Gras-related words are the hardest hit. Take *krewe*, for example. The computer informs me that *krewe* is not a word and suggests I use *crewel* instead. A cruel suggestion indeed.

Even *Mardi Gras* itself is illegal. *Mardi* does not exist, and *Gras* is allowed only as an acronym for "Generally Recognized As Safe," an FDA phrase used on food labels. Anyone who believes that Mardi Gras is "generally recognized as safe" has not crawled Bourbon Street at the stroke of midnight after a long Carnival Day.

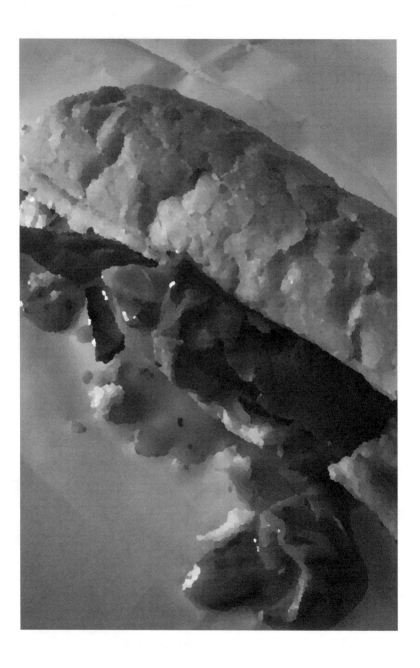

The computer also wants to argue about parts of speech. *Throws* is listed only as an action verb, as in "Drew Brees throws the perfect pass and wins the Super Bowl!" However, according to the computer, *throws* cannot be used as a noun, as in "Revelers returned home with armloads of Mardi Gras throws after the parade." I'm confident that the revelers would beg to differ.

Conversely, *second line* is allowed only as an adjective/noun set, as in "She drew a first line, and then she drew a second line." Ho-hum. It is not allowed as an action verb, as in "The revelers second-lined down St. Charles Avenue to the stirring sounds of St. Aug's Marching 100." Okay, how much more action do you need than that?

Plan to eat your kingcake on the neutral ground? The computer is willing to work with you on this one. First, you must break *kingcake* into two words. *King. Cake.* Second, you'll have to accept the assertion that "neutral ground" does not involve a street or the median down its middle. If you are willing to accept these terms, the grammar check is more than happy to allow you to have a cake baked by a male sovereign and to allow you to eat said cake—but only in neutral Switzerland and only as long as you're not standing on a strip of ground between two sides of a street.

As if assaults on Mardi Gras lingo were not bad enough, take a look at what the computer has to say about the lexicon of our cuisine. Want your po-boy dressed? The grammar check will not allow it. First, the word *po-boy* does not exist. The computer suggests *potboy* instead, with *pool boy* listed as another suggestion. And *dressed?* Apparently, the only food that can be "dressed" is a salad. Nothing like a healthy green dressed potboy for lunch, eh? Then again, we could always order a pool boy instead—dressed or undressed.

Want an erster po-boy with mynez? The computer suggests you try Ester with mynas instead. Tell *that* to the potboy!

Debris is defined as "wreckage," "flotsam," or "something that has been destroyed." Yeah, you could say we've been there, done that. But there is no definition for *debris* as a sandwich ingredient. So, the next time you order a Ferdi with debris at Mother's, be sure to pick out and discard the flotsam before taking your first bite.

Love stuffed mirliton? That might be kind of difficult. At first glance, *mirliton* appears not to be a word at all, as it is not recognized by the computer. However, further research for more obscure meanings reveals that a mirliton is a type of kazoo or eunuch flute, a hussar hat, and an almond tartlet. Try stuffing one of those with shrimp and ham.

Though you might find turducken on your table at Thanksgiving, you won't find it in the computer's dictionary or thesaurus. Further research reveals you are eating "whole stuffed camel" instead. Yum!

If your palate is not tickled by flotsam potboys, eunuch flutes, and camel, how about a bowl of thick, rich étouffée? Aw, sorry, out of luck again, cap. Apparently, there's no such thing as étouffée. But you could sample some good, hearty crawfish toffee. Or perhaps a generous helping of shrimp toupee. Oops, waiter? Over here, please. There's a hair in my toupee étouffée.

Do you prefer your boudin steamed so that the casing comes out soft? Or would you rather it broiled so that it comes out crispy? Well, actually, never mind. You can't have any. The computer has a real problem with boudin. Luckily, you can have boudoir instead. So I guess the question becomes: do you prefer your boudoir steamy or broiling? Ooh, la, la!

If you plan to finish off your meal with a good thick slice of doberge, think again. Try instead for its Americanized spelling, *dobash,* and you still get nothing but a mouthful of wavy red lines. Neither *doberge* nor *dobash* exists. Not to worry, however. The computer suggests that you try some delicious *dob ash* for dessert.

Unfortunately, if you want some coffee with your dob ash, café au lait will be out of the question. Actually, *café* is allowed. And *au* is okay. (*Au* is okay?!) But there's a real glitch with the *lait.* Instead of café au lait, you'll have to opt for café au laity (coffee with non-clergymen), café au late (coffee after midnight), or café au laid (uh, no comment on that last option).

If you're looking for a rousing game of bourré (or bourrée) after dinner, leave the cards at home and bring a lot of liquor instead. The computer won't allow a card game, but consult a French dictionary and you'll find that bourré is a colloquialism for "drunk" or "sloshed." Hooray! This problem is fixable. Just make sure you "bottoms up" before you "ante up," and France won't give you any problems.

The New Orleans Saints fare no better than the rest of us. Let's take, for example, the "dat" in Who Dat. There may be a whole nation of us Who Dats, but apparently we have to agree to change our name to the Who Dots, the Who Dads, or the Who Dams. Actually, I kinda like the last suggestion. Picture it: a Hail Mary pass lands right in the hands of a wide-open Saints receiver. He's at the thirty, the twenty, the ten. Touchdown! Seventy thousand delirious Black-and-Gold fans jump to their feet and let loose with a rousing "Who Dam!" Oh, yeah!

Unfortunately, though, the Saints may have to rethink their trademark emblem, the fleur de lis. *Fleur* doesn't get a red wavy underline; nor does *de,* even though neither is listed in the computer dictionary. However, my laptop brings out the red ink for the *lis.* Surely, I meant *fleur de lips,* it tells me. Or *fleur de leis,* if I happened to be in Honolulu. But no self-respecting Who Dat would stand for a 300-pound Saints defensive back sporting bright red fleur de lips on his jersey or multicolored fleur de leis on his helmet. So "Who Dam!" to that!

But whether they're wearing lips or leis, at least the Saints exist. The Chalmatians are not so lucky. No such thing as a Chalmatian? Just wait 'til I tell Mawmaw and Pawpaw when they get back from making groceries out in da parish.

And now, the biggest insult of all, the one that should make every New Orleanian rise up in angry protest: *Orleanian* doesn't exist. Not allowed. Forbidden. Red, wavy line.

New Orleanians don't exist?! Enough is enough. We have to draw the line somewhere (and I don't mean a wavy one!), and this is it! Time to tell those computer companies where they can put their fleur de lips.

Are you with me, my fellow yats?

Oops, I mean, *yaks.*

Shell Games

We should have known from the moment he walked in that this was going to be a show to remember. We were seated at a lakefront restaurant that specialized in boiled seafood served on a plastic tray on a table covered with newspapers, and in he walked wearing a fancy white dinner suit. He followed the waitress toward his table but stopped halfway there. He had just noticed the rhythmic rocking of the restaurant, which rested on piers several feet above the surface of the lake. A puzzled look crossed his face, as if he were trying to decide whether he was imagining the swaying or actually feeling it. With arms outstretched and a wide stride, he walked gingerly to his table.

The waitress handed him a menu and left. We could hear him struggle through some of the words. "Ee-too-fee," he pronounced out loud, then shook his head with a puzzled look. "Court-bullion," and another shake of the head. "Bis-cue?"

I was just about to go over and clue him in when the waitress approached his table and asked for his order.

"Well," he said, "I think I'll skip these fancy dishes and stick with the plain seafood instead. I see that everything comes by the dozen, so I'll take a dozen crabs, a dozen crawfish, a dozen shrimp, and a dozen oysters."

The waitress looked up from her pad. "Will the rest of your party be arriving soon, sir?"

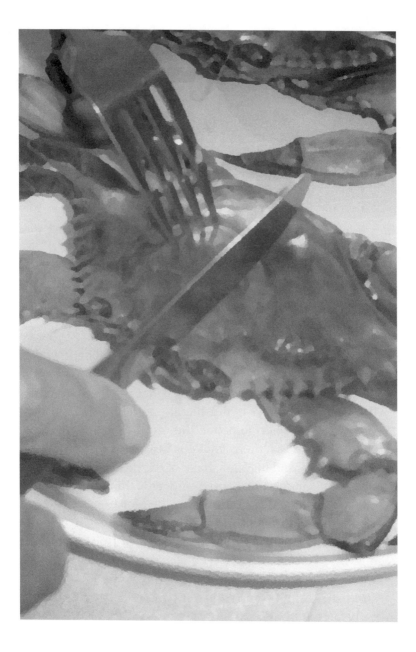

"Oh, no. I'm eating alone."

"I see," the waitress said, nodding. "Would you like your oysters fried or on the half-shell?"

"Actually, I want the whole shell. And bring tartar sauce for my fish."

The waitress paused. "What fish?"

"The crawfish," he responded, beaming. "And I assume you'll remove the heads and tails before serving them."

"But sir," the waitress started. Then she caught our eye. By this time, my tablemates and I had given up on trying to stifle the giggles. She shrugged her shoulders, then answered, "Yes, sir, we'll remove the heads and tails from the crawfish for you."

A few minutes later, the waitress returned with his tray. She set it down in front of him and he scrutinized its contents. It was obviously not what he had expected: twelve whole crabs with lots of little legs sticking out from the sides (not the big long crab legs—sans bodies—that he was probably used to having at Red Lobster), twelve shrimp, twelve dirty gray rocks, and twelve little plops of tartar sauce with nothing under them.

His confidence was a bit shaken. The waitress paused while he looked over his meal.

"Perhaps I can give you a few tips on how to shell each of these," she offered.

The man glanced around and caught us looking in his direction. He shook his head and turned down her offer of help in a voice purposely loud enough for us to hear. "Yankee ingenuity," he said tapping his forefinger to his temple. "I'm sure I can figure it out myself." Then he waved her away.

The intrepid diner picked up his knife and fork and paused, turning his attention to the boiled crabs first. Putting the tines of the fork to the back of a crab, he began sawing away with his knife in an attempt to cut through the hard shell. Almost immediately, the knife slid off the back of the crab.

More and more pressure on the knife only made it slide off with more force and noise. He knew he was beginning to attract attention. Yes, one of us should have gone over at this point and helped him, but then we reminded ourselves that he had already turned down an offer of help. Besides, think of the entertainment we would miss if he accepted our offer.

Turning the crustacean over, he applied the knife to the belly side of the crab and . . . *crunch!* He looked up beaming. Now he was getting somewhere. He looked over at us with a victorious smile, and we smiled back. He began to pick off the small pieces of cracked shell, bit by bit, losing much of the crabmeat in the process. When a small circle had been cleared in the belly of the beast, he began to dig through the insides with a spoon, prying up a chunk that actually contained a fair amount of crabmeat. He put it into his mouth and crunched, then began spitting out piece after piece of the inside shells. Having now dug all the way through to the hard back shell of the crab, he finally came upon some gray feathery meat that was still intact. Unaware that he was about to eat the dead man's fingers (the crab's gills), he triumphantly plopped them into his mouth and began to chew through a smile. A smile that quickly vanished. With real determination, he managed to swallow that little biteful. We had to give it to him: he was determined. Apparently, however, determination can taste pretty nasty sometimes.

Next, he turned to the shrimp. Knowing the head and tail had to come off, he used his knife and fork to saw off both ends of the first shrimp. Unfortunately, much of the body came off along with the two ends. Next, he amputated the legs—again with his knife and fork—and again lost a good portion of the mutilated creature in the process. After peeling the pitiful little inch-long piece of shrimp that was left, he popped it into his mouth. He looked up at us, and we gave him the thumbs up. He finished off the other eleven shrimp in the same manner. The meat gleaned from all of them would have barely qualified as a snack, much less a meal, but he smiled proudly at his success.

Next, he turned his attention to the oysters, and we held our collective breath. This was gonna be good. Through some stroke of genius he tried to insert the knife into the edges of the shell and started prying, applying more and more force. The blade broke. We peeked in his direction and saw him wrapping his napkin around his hand, tending to a nasty cut across the palm. Undeterred, he began to pound on the shell with the handle of the knife. Oyster-shell chips flew to nearby tables. We tried to pretend we were not aware of his futile attempts and barely managed not to laugh out loud. When the noise and oyster chips stopped, we stole a peek in his direction. He surreptitiously slid one of the oysters under the front leg of his chair; then he plopped down hard in his seat. The oyster went flying across the floor.

He was now the center of attention of the entire restaurant. The giggles at the surrounding tables turned to guffaws. It was no use trying restraint at this point.

He searched for the last seafood item on the platter. But there was nothing of the headless, tailless crawfish to find. Only twelve memorial piles of tartar sauce.

Finally, guilt got the better of us, and I walked over to his table. "I'll be glad to help you with the rest of the crabs," I offered.

He put his bandaged hand to his stomach and answered, "Oh, no, thanks, I'm quite full now."

"I see," I replied. "I'm glad you enjoyed your meal."

"Thanks for your kindness," he said. "I guess it's true what they say about Southern hospitality."

Okay, yes, I felt a twinge of guilt.

Then he caught me by the elbow, and his voice dropped to a whisper. "Uh, hey, I, uh, am supposed to meet an acquaintance at a Burger King in this area," he said. "For coffee," he was quick to add.

"Burger King," I repeated. "For coffee."

He nodded, and I named a nearby intersection where he'd find a Burger King.

For coffee.

"Thanks," he said, plopping a few large bills on the table as he got up to leave. He tipped an imaginary hat to my friends still seated around our table, and they returned the courtesy with smiles and a friendly wave. He continued toward the exit, pausing only momentarily at the "Y'all come back" sign, and then walked out the door toward a waiting cab.

Neaux Sneaux

Santa always came through for me when I was a child growing up in Gentilly. Still, I somehow felt deprived of the Christmas experience as a whole.

"Dashing through the snow . . . ?" Nope, never happened.
"A sleighing song . . . ?" Never got to sing one.
"Treetops glistening . . . ?" Not that *I* ever saw.

As the years passed, however, I learned to count my blessings. A white Christmas Day is a grand idea, but not if it means enduring the hundred other days of brutal cold that come with it. In fact, I think that most of us would have to admit that, yes, we do occasionally take some malicious pleasure in watching weather reports of people up North who spend a good part of their Christmas morning scraping ice off of windshields in subfreezing temperatures, sliding and crashing on slick city streets, and snow-blowing paths to their doors as the icicles on their noses grow longer and longer. By comparison, a balmy local Christmas is just fine. It still gets cold enough once in a while to make it "feel" like Christmas. And if we just *must* frolic in the white stuff, we can always drive on over to City Park and get in line for the annual snow dump.

Thus, while we do indeed celebrate the "reason for the season" along with everyone in the country, what they celebrate and what we celebrate are poles apart. Take note:

What They Celebrate	What We Celebrate
Santa Claus	Papa Noel
Caroling in the snow	Caroling in Jackson Square
Bing Crosby	Benny Grunch
Hot cider and figgy pudding	Café au lait and bread pudding in rum sauce
"The Twelve Days of Christmas"	"The Twelve Yats of Christmas" (à la Benny G.)
Walking through a winter wonderland	Walking through the lobby of the Roosevelt
Rudolph's red nose to guide Santa	Bonfires on the levee to guide Papa Noel
One-horse open sleigh	Lighted, bedecked streetcars
Kris Kringle	Mr. Bingle
Chestnuts roasting on an open fire	Satsumas arriving from Plaquemines Parish
Frequent snow, sleet, and slush	A scheduled snow day in City Park
Bloomingdale's Christmas window displays	Al Copeland's lights
Santa in a sleigh	Papa Noel in a pirogue

And for lagniappe, we get the last laugh. When Christmas and New Year's are over, when the tree comes down and the decorations get packed away, where does that leave everybody? Elsewhere, the end of the holiday season signals the start of the coldest, bleakest part of winter and the beginning of the post-holiday blues. Here, the end of the holiday season marks the start of the Mardi Gras season: balls, parties, costume planning, and kingcakes.

So, heaux-heaux-heaux—and vive la difference!

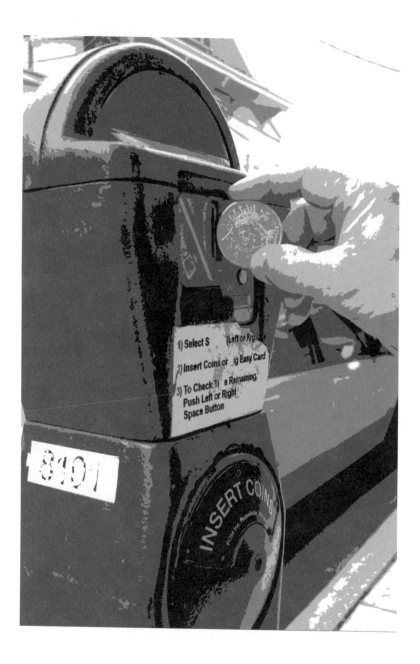

1) Select S   (Left or Rig...

2) Insert Coins or ...g Easy Card

3) To Check Ti...e Remaining,
   Push Left or Right
   Space Button

INSERT COINS

Mardi Gras Recycled

Remember that plastic pearl necklace you caught off the 159th float in the Elks Krewe of Orleanians last year—the necklace that you wanted more than anything else in the world, the necklace for which you were ready to risk life and limb, the necklace that gave you the Thrill of the Grab? Well, it's now sitting somewhere in your attic along with 472 other plastic necklaces that you were willing to crawl on your hands and knees for and thirty-nine parade cups that brought you such great joy. And that's on top of the leftovers from a dozen other Carnivals.

Well, you're not alone. In fact, let's face it. We're a city of Mardi Gras pack rats.

While people around the country are jumping on the recycling bandwagon to do their part for Mother Earth, residents in these parts are faced with a unique problem. Not only do we have to recycle old throwaways like aluminum cans and glass, we also have to figure out what to do with a yearly influx of several tons of plastic beads, a few million doubloons, and enough plastic cups to set every table in the Northern Hemisphere.

In the past, Mardi Gras recycling meant "save it all" just in case an acquaintance would be riding in a truck parade the next year. That way, the rider could re-throw the trinkets someone else threw the previous year.

But, hey, some of this stuff needs to be retired. I've caught the exact same pair of ugly purple-and-brown beads with a broken clasp for three years in a row.

So, let's get creative with our Mardi Gras leftovers. For example:

⚜ How about using truckloads of leftover beads for landfill instead of using truckloads of spillway sand? Not only would this get rid of tons of throws, it would solve the city's sinkage problem at the same time. Forget about pumping spillway sand beneath cracking slabs. Pump beads under there instead! Entire neighborhoods could be saved from sinking deeper and deeper into the swamps upon which they were built.

Imagine the field day this would give future archaeologists. Centuries pass. The year is now 2392. Mardi Gras beads aren't thrown from floats anymore. (They are automatically credited to your Carnival account while you watch virtual parade graphics via Internet linkups.)

What would the scientists of the future say about a long-gone society that built its houses on a bedrock of jewels?

⚜ Or maybe the New Orleans Streets Department could use the beads as pothole filler. After being crushed and mixed with melted tar, recycled throws would provide an inexhaustible supply of material for the city's inexhaustible supply of bottomless pits that pockmark our streets.

⚜ The city could alter downtown parking meters, adding a special slot that would accept doubloons. This method of feeding the meters would give the natives a financial break and loosen up the bottleneck in Traffic Court.

❧ Schedule a yearly Sargi Dram, i.e., a backwards Mardi Gras. On Ash Wednesday morning, the parades would pass again. But this time, float riders would have to beg for beads from the people in the streets.

The positive psychological effects for lowly parade-goers could be enormous. As krewe members shout, "Throw me something, Mister" from their floats, the people lining the parade route could taunt the riders by displaying huge clumps of tangled beads, then slowly extricate one measly strand, toss it to the groveling beggars on the floats, and watch them fight for it.

Turnabout is fair play.

❧ Melt down purple, green, and gold aluminum doubloons and use them to plate the Huey P. Long Bridge so it doesn't have to be sand-blasted and repainted every year. A purple, green, and gold bridge? Why not? There'd be no more worries about rust, and the bridge would serve as a fitting monument to our favorite holiday.

❧ Encourage a new holiday tradition for New Orleans families during the Christmas season. When it's time to decorate the tree, family members can string together Mardi Gras necklaces to create one long strand, which would then be used instead of tacky garland to loop around the tree. Why pay for tasteless decorations when you can get them for free?

❧ Save our coast! Link used doubloons together like chainmail to create a metal barrier for our wetlands to prevent coastal erosion and reinforce the levees. Lay football-field-sized blankets of interlocked doubloons over disappearing marshes to hold them in place. Place wide sheets of linked doubloons on each side of the levees to armor them. From Cocodrie to Grand Isle to Venice, we've got you covered!

✤ And why not use the throws to boost tourism? Start a citywide campaign to fill Mardi Gras cups with beads and doubloons, and then send these care packages to random people around the country. Explain in an enclosed note that if they come to the Mardi Gras next year, they'll get bag-loads of the stuff for free. (It would be wise not to mention in the note that the "free" beads come with the exorbitant cost of a four-night minimum stay at an expensive downtown hotel.)

✤ Once the world has been saturated with Mardi Gras throws, pack the leftovers into unmanned rockets and jettison them into deep space. If it works for nuclear waste, it'll work for Mardi Gras beads.

I sure hope that purple-and-brown necklace with the broken clasp is on the first flight out of here.

A Return to "Romper Room"

. . . And now, boys and girls, New Orleans public television station WYAT is proud to bring you your favorite morning program: "Romper Room."

"Good morning, children! My name is Miss Debbie. Welcome to 'Romper Room.' Please take a seat at your desks, and we will get started. Uh, yes, Michelle, I see your hand up, like a good little Do-Bee. Do you have a question to share with us?"

Michelle nodded. "I'm really confused about something, Miss Debbie," she began shyly. "You see, I have a Web pal in Ohio. Her name is Janet. And Janet said she doesn't kiss strange men marching down the street just so she can get a paper flower."

There was a gasp from all of the other good little Do-Bees in the classroom. "That's a sad thing, isn't it, children?" asked Miss Debbie. The children nodded.

Michelle continued. "Janet said *none* of her friends kiss strange men so they can get paper flowers. So I asked her, 'If you don't kiss the marchers, how do you get purple, green, and gold paper flowers?'" Michelle paused, and a look of pity crossed her young face before she went on. "Janet said she doesn't have any paper flowers, and even worse, she doesn't

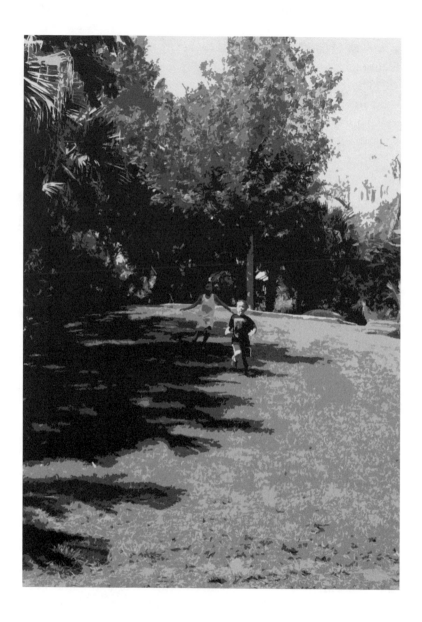

want any paper flowers!" In disbelief she looked up at her teacher. "Could that really be true, Miss Debbie? Doesn't everybody want purple, green, and gold paper flowers to wear in their hair on Mardi Gras day?"

Perplexed, the children turned to Miss Debbie, anxiously awaiting her answer.

"Oh, my good little Do-Bees," responded the kindly teacher, "I know it must be hard for you to understand this at your age, but children who live in other cities don't want purple, green, and gold paper flowers because they don't know how special those flowers are."

"Why not?" asked the little yats.

"Because they don't know how special Mardi Gras is."

"Why not?" came the chorus again.

Miss Debbie took a deep breath before continuing. "Because, my darlings, most children in the world have never been to Mardi Gras."

There was stunned silence on the set. Then some of the children began to cry.

"I'm afraid it's true, boys and girls. Most other places don't have Mardi Gras at all. And none of them have a Mardi Gras like we do."

The children shook their heads sadly. Then Darrell raised his hand. "But, Miss Debbie," he said, "what do the other people in the world do on Mardi Gras day?"

Miss Debbie shrugged her shoulders. "Just the ordinary things they do on other days, I guess. They go to school or go to work."

Michelle pondered the implications of this fact, and her expression softened. "Well, then, Miss Debbie, I'm not mad at Janet anymore," she decided. "I guess I just feel sorry for her."

The good little Do-Bees nodded their heads in agreement. But the room was full of sadness for the other children in the world.

Miss Debbie knew she had to brighten the mood. "I have an idea, boys and girls. Let's have parade practice, shall we?"

The somber atmosphere immediately dissipated, and the children bounced up and down at their desks with excitement. Miss Debbie breathed a sigh of relief.

"Okay, everyone, pretend you are sitting in your seat on top of a ladder at a parade with your mommy or daddy standing behind you. And, oh, look! There's a float coming down the street! Let's see those parade faces now. Remember, pleading and expectant. Pleading and expectant. Ah, very good! And don't forget that irresistible smile. Big smile now. Show some teeth—if you still have them, I mean. Good, good! All right, now, eyes open wide in anticipation. Wider, wider! Excellent, children!" said Miss Debbie. The children clapped for themselves.

"Okay, now, the float is getting closer. Hands up, hands up! And let's have a big 'Hey, Mister!'"

"Hey, Mister!" the children shouted.

"I can't *hear* you!" said Miss Debbie in a drill sergeant's singsongy voice.

"Hey, Mister!" they shouted louder. "Throw me something, Mister!"

"That's more like it!" praised Miss Debbie, and the children beamed at her approval. "Now let's practice 'catch and stash.' Are you ready?"

The children nodded and sat up straight.

"Okay, imagine you've just caught some beads. Show me what you do next."

Miss Debbie watched proudly as the children transferred their pretend beads to their right hands and gave a quick thank-you wave with their left hands as they stashed the catch in the pretend bag tied to the side of the pretend ladder. Then they got both hands back up in the wink of an eye. "Bravo, bravo, my darlings!" said Miss Debbie. "Okay, the float has passed, and the next is a half-block away. Who can tell me what you do now?"

Twenty hands went up. "Okay, Lela, you tell the class."

"We make sure all the beads are put away in the bag so the riders on the next float will think we haven't caught much, and they'll feel sorry for us, and they'll throw more stuff to us."

The children cheered. "Wonderful!" said Miss Debbie. "Wasn't that fun?" Then she continued, "Okay, let's leave Mardi Gras for a while and talk about something else. Who would like to tell the class what they did on their summer vacation?" Five hands shot up. "Okay, Johnny, let's start with you."

Johnny stood up. "I went on vacation to visit my cousin," he said. "And where he lives there were these big things coming out of the ground, and they were really, really big, and we even drove over them. It was so weird; when you were on one side of these things you couldn't see what was on the other side until you got to the top of the thing and you could look down on what was on the other side of it."

"Ah," said Miss Debbie. "Mountains."

"Yeah, that's what Bobby's dad called them."

"They're sort of like Monkey Hill in Audubon Park, but much, much bigger," Miss Debbie offered, trying as best she could to explain the concept of "mountain" to the other children in the class.

Johnny nodded. "Yeah, sort of. But why did they put them in the middle of the highway? At least when we roll down Monkey Hill, we don't have to worry about ending up in the middle of a street."

The children turned to each other and nodded in agreement. "That would be really dangerous, wouldn't it?" asked Miss Debbie. The Do-Bees nodded again. "Only Don't-Bees go in the street without Mommy or Daddy," she reminded them.

"And guess what they had in their house, Miss Debbie!" shouted Johnny. "A celery!"

"A celery?" she asked.

"Yeah, there was a door in one of their walls and when you opened the door, there were stairs, and the stairs went down to the celery. It was like a room under the ground. Celeries are for ping-pong tables. How come we don't have celeries in New Orleans?"

Miss Debbie smiled. "The word is 'cellar,' darling," she corrected gently. Then she explained to the little children the geological facts of life for a city below sea level. The children listened with rapt attention and took the news fairly well, considering that many of them had just come to the heartbreaking realization that they would never have a ping-pong table.

Little Johnny shuffled his feet; then he looked away wistfully. Miss Debbie's maternal instinct picked up the signal. "There's something else you need to tell the class, isn't there, sweetie?" she asked.

Johnny lowered his head and nodded. Then he took a deep breath and started into his story. "Bobby's family and I stopped at a restaurant on our trip. Everybody else told the waitress what they wanted, and then it was my turn to order. I asked for a hamburger. Then I told her I wanted it dressed. The waitress just looked at me and everyone got quiet, and then Bobby's bratty little sister said real loud so the whole restaurant could hear: 'Well, I hope you weren't going to eat it while you were naked!' And then everyone laughed at me."

Some of the children in the class laughed too when they heard the word "naked."

"All right, that's enough, class," chastised Miss Debbie. Then she turned to Johnny. "Oh, my poor darling," she said, shaking her head. "Other people in the world don't know what 'dressed' means. But try to look on the bright side. Other people in the world don't know how good a po-boy tastes either—dressed or not—because they don't even have po-boys!"

"They don't?" the class asked in unison. Miss Debbie shook her head. Johnny seemed to brighten up a little. "I guess I'd rather get laughed at just once than live my whole life without po-boys," he reasoned wisely. His classmates nodded in agreement.

"And guess what else," Miss Debbie said in a conspiratorial tone. "The other children don't know how to peel crawfish. But you do, don't you?"

The children nodded vigorously.

"Okay, let's pretend there is a pile of crawfish in front of you. Show me what you do."

Each of the children picked up an imaginary crawfish and pulled off the imaginary head. Some of the children sucked the heads; others tossed them to the side. Miss Debbie could tell who the real pros were. Then all of them peeled the tail. Most of the girls removed the vein down the back. Most of the boys just tossed the whole thing in their mouths.

"Oh, no!" shouted Michael, holding up his imaginary crawfish. "I have a straight tail!"

"Throw it back! Throw it back!" the children shouted in alarm.

Then the class laughed. Jessica raised her hand. "Miss

Debbie, if the other children don't know how to peel crawfish, then what do they do at a crawfish boil?" she asked.

Miss Debbie smiled coyly. "They don't have crawfish boils," she answered in a whisper. The class drew in a collective breath, then applauded. Secretly, Miss Debbie wondered if she had crossed the line. Raising young yats is a complex balancing act. Miss Debbie knew that after pointing out that other people have things that we don't (like cellars), it would be important to emphasize that other people don't have things that we *do* (like crawfish boils). She knew that the scale was tipped heavily in our favor. Still, nice Do-Bees don't gloat. She hoped she had handled the balancing act appropriately, and she knew it was time to switch gears.

"Okay, children, time for our vocabulary lesson," she announced. "Has anyone heard a new word to tell the class about?"

"My uncle said he took a subway," volunteered Darlene. "What's a subway?"

Ooh, this was going to be a tough one, Miss Debbie thought. *How do you explain a foreign concept like "subway" to young yats who've never even seen a tunnel?* She knew she would have to get creative. Then it came to her. "Okay, children, I want you to imagine a really, really long 'celery' under the streets of New Orleans. In fact, this celery crisscrosses under the whole city, from uptown to Gentilly to Metairie to New Orleans East and everyplace in between."

"What about the West Bank?" asked David.

"And Chalmette?" asked Kelly.

Miss Debbie nodded. "Yes, yes. This long underground celery goes everywhere. Now, picture a long string of St. Charles Avenue streetcars connected together and racing at warp speed through the celery." The children nodded; they understood. *Voila!* she thought proudly. *A subway—New Orleans style.*

Jamie raised her hand. "I heard the Weather Channel say there was a blizzard. What's a blizzard?"

Miss Debbie looked around at the expectant faces of her pupils. How could she convey the full force and impact of "blizzard" when most of these little ones had never seen actual snow or—at best—only a rare dusting of gentle powder? "Okay, children, I want you to picture all the sno-ball machines in the city, lots and lots and lots of them, from Plum Street and Sal's and Hansen's and Casey's and every other sno-ball stand in the city. Now picture all these sno-ball machines attached to the inside roof of the Superdome, cranking out sno-ball ice as fast as they can. Really, really fast. Now remember, there is no strawberry syrup on the sno-balls. Then I want you to picture a small hurricane whirling inside the Dome at the same time; it is a very, very small hurricane, but it is blowing the sno-ball snow around really hard. Can you picture it?" she asked.

"Yes," they replied, and she breathed a sigh of relief. Thank goodness she had been able to help them understand. Miss Debbie was happy to see that there were only a few more minutes left in today's show.

"Okay, whose turn is it today to tell the class what you want to be when you grow up?" she asked.

Teresa raised her hand tentatively. "It's my turn, Miss Debbie," she said in a very quiet voice. "But I'm afraid to tell you, because you might laugh at me like my cousin in California did."

Miss Debbie put her hand on Teresa's shoulder. "Of course I won't laugh. Neither will the class. Okay?"

Teresa nodded her head. "I want to be a maid when I grow up," she said.

"Me, too! Me, too!" shouted some of the other girls.

"See? We think that's a wonderful thing. Why did your cousin laugh at you?" Miss Debbie asked.

"Well, when I told her I wanted to be a maid, she said it was the stupidest idea ever—that nobody *wants* to be a maid when they grow up. But *I* do!" Teresa said, her eyes growing brighter and her voice stronger. "And I'm going to have the sparkliest tiara ever and the fanciest gown with lots and lots of rhinestones and the handsomest duke to walk me around the ballroom floor!"

Miss Debbie clapped her hands in excitement for her student. "That will be wonderful, Teresa. You will be a beautiful maid."

The children clapped in agreement. Miss Debbie was so proud of her little yats. They had taken on some difficult topics today, and they had handled them so well.

"Well, boys and girls, our show is over for today. You have all been wonderful little Do-Bees. Now wave goodbye to our viewers while I look through my magic mirror at all the good Do-Bees at home. I see Angela and Bernice and Trey, Ivy, and Greg. Thank you so much for watching our show today. We'll see you all again tomorrow."

Season According to Taste

A long time ago, ancient astronomers divided the year into four neat little packages called seasons, whose beginnings and endings were determined by solstices, equinoxes, and other mystical joggings of the sun.

Here in New Orleans, however, the four prescribed seasons have little relevance. Summer starts sometime in March and hangs around until October. Our only other season is "rest-of-the-year."

But not to worry. If this city has been cheated out of the proper meteorological seasons, it has instead been blessed with its own gastronomical seasons. We define our times of the year by the foods we eat.

It all starts on January 6 with kingcake season. The beginning of this season is marked by an eagerness to try new varieties and sample old favorites. And what fun to get the piece with the baby! But after several weeks of indulging, we begin to avoid the purple, green, and gold oversized doughnut like the plague, and most of us would sell our souls for Superman's X-ray vision if it would keep us from picking the one fateful slice that will hit us in the wallet.

How appropriate that kingcake season culminates on *Fat* Tuesday, especially if your weakness happens to be the cream-cheese-filled variety. In fact, Carnival Day is truly a

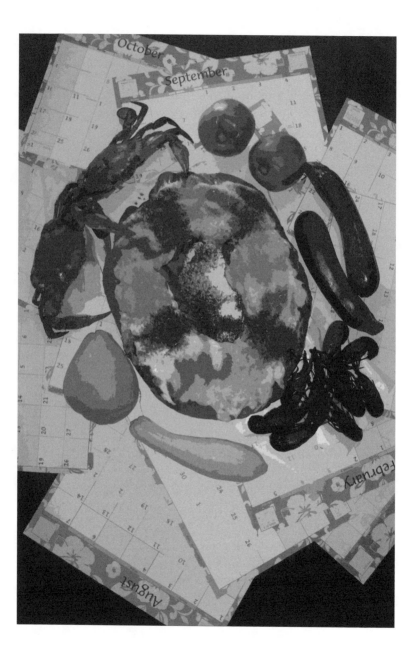

food season unto itself. Witness the mountain of empty fried-chicken boxes and discarded beer cans at parades. Finally, as Mardi Gras draws to a close, the parade-weary, traffic-stressed, kingcake-bloated population of New Orleans is relieved to welcome the onset of the next season—Lent.

Forty days of abstinence, penance, and sacrifice. Sort of. Of course, the idea of abstinence is to give up something we like. However, we have a poor record when it comes to the sackcloth-and-ashes concept. While Catholics in the rest of the country give up their Friday-night steaks and suffer through fish sticks and tuna casseroles, we "suffer" through crawfish by the sackload.

Some penance. Surely it is nothing short of Divine Providence that crawfish season and the Lenten season overlap. Amen!

As crawfish season nears its end, another delicacy arrives on its heels: the first Creole tomatoes hit grocery-store shelves. After too many months of eating plastic California tomatoes, local consumers gratefully pick up the much uglier but gastronomically superior Creole variety, and they drool as they sigh, "Aren't these just beautiful?" Proof positive that beauty is indeed in the eye of the beholder.

With King Creole, the season of vegetables has arrived. We cheer the abundance of plentiful zucchinis and mirlitons. Several weeks later, we curse the abundance of plentiful zucchinis and mirlitons.

Fortunately, just when we think the city will smother under a mountain of squash, the sno-ball season hits its peak. And sno-balls are serious stuff. In fact, if you want to liven up a dull dinner party, ask your tablemates to agree on the best sno-ball stand in the city.

By the time the argument ends, the first wave of cool

weather is here, and we're into the oyster season.

Few people maintain an indifferent attitude about raw oysters. For some, there's nothing as appetizing as slurping down a moist mollusk drenched in ketchup and horseradish. For others, it is akin to ingesting syrup of ipecac. But even if you're one of those who loves 'em on the half-shell, after several weeks, it's time for a change. That's why the Pilgrims scheduled Thanksgiving when they did—so that we could enjoy oyster dressing with our Thanksgiving turkey.

Soon we're in the midst of the sweets season. Between the whirlwind of holiday parties and plethora of home-baked gifts, the city's collective sweet tooth rides a sugary high: pralines, pecan fudge, doberge, Italian cream cake, pecan pie, divinity, and bread pudding with rum sauce. The year is about to end, as it began, on a sweet note.

As the New Year's baby descends during the countdown to the new year, you can bet local bakeries are already stocking up on tiny plastic kingcake dolls.

Loosen your belts. The entire round of New Orleans seasons is about to start all over again.

Lies That New Orleans Parents Tell Their Children

Despite everything we preach to our children about the importance of character, honesty, and integrity, admit it: we've all lied to our children at some point or other.

And since New Orleans parents face a special set of challenges raising children in this city, they also have a special repertoire of lies to help them cope—some little white fibs, some real whoppers. Take, for example, the following untruths.

It's not that I don't *want* to peel all your crawfish for you. It's just that, well, the rule is that once a person turns seven years old, they're supposed to peel for themselves. So go practice and leave Daddy alone to eat his own crawfish.

~~~~~~~~~~~~

No, we don't need to take Fluffy and Elmo with us when we evacuate. Hamsters and lizards are great swimmers.

~~~~~~~~~~~~

Quit bugging me. The sno-ball stand is not open for the summer yet. I promise I'll take you as soon as it opens.

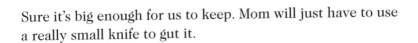

Sure it's big enough for us to keep. Mom will just have to use a really small knife to gut it.

~~~~~~~~~~~

Quit bugging me. The sno-ball stand is already closed for the winter. I promise I'll take you as soon as it opens in the spring.

~~~~~~~~~~~

If the Tooth Fairy left you doubloons instead of quarters, there's nothing *I* can do about it.

~~~~~~~~~~~

Don't worry. Santa Claus can land his sleigh on our roof even if there isn't any snow up there.

~~~~~~~~~~~

Popeye's is closed on Wednesdays. You'll have to take a PB&J for your field-trip lunch today.

~~~~~~~~~~~

Yes, darling, I'm praying just as hard as you are that it will snow tomorrow.

~~~~~~~~~~~

Yes, darling, I'm praying just as hard as you are that they will cancel school today because of those five snowflakes that made it all the way to the ground before melting.

~~~~~~~~~~~

Did you know that Daddy was at that very first Saints game when John Gilliam returned the opening kick on the first Saints play ever and ran it in for a touchdown?

~~~~~~~~~~~

Yes, dear, I know it's real bumpy riding down our street. That's because of all the potholes, but the New Orleans Streets Department will be here to fix them very soon.

~~~~~~~~~~~

Did you know that Daddy was at that Saints game when Tom Dempsey kicked the longest field goal ever?

~~~~~~~~~~~

You can't finish a $2.50-size sno-ball. The $1 size is perfect for you.

~~~~~~~~~~~

Yes, I know that Mommy gave up chocolate for Lent. But it's okay for me to eat this Elmer's Gold Brick Egg today because it's Sunday. Sundays don't count in Lent.

~~~~~~~~~~~

I wish I *could* make it cooler in here, but the AC is already on its coldest setting. The thermostat doesn't have any numbers lower than seventy-six.

~~~~~~~~~~~

No, darling, your pleated, plaid wool school-uniform skirt does not make you look fat.

~~~~~~~~~~~

It's not that I *mind* spending an extra $100 for a flocked tree. It's just that you can't recycle flocked trees to help save the wetlands, so we'll go with this regular green one instead.

~~~~~~~~~~~

Yes, a Chalmatian is just like any other New Orleanian.

~~~~~~~~~~~

Why waste an extra fifty cents? A sno-ball *without* condensed milk is just as good as one *with* condensed milk.

~~~~~~~~~~~

I don't care *what* Uncle Larry said. I did not get my driver's license before I was seventeen, and neither will you!

~~~~~~~~~~~

No, the crabs don't mind when I put them in the boiling water.

~~~~~~~~~~~

I don't care *what* Uncle Larry said. I did not drink alcohol before I was twenty-one, and neither will you!

~~~~~~~~~~~

Of course, son. The Tulane Green Wave has beaten LSU many, many times.

~~~~~~~~~~~

I don't care *what* Uncle Larry said. I have never gone to a strip club on Bourbon Street, and neither will you!

~~~~~~~~~~~

And the lie that we can remove from our repertoire:

I wouldn't get my hopes up too high if I were you. The Saints will never make it to the Super Bowl, and if they do, there's no way they'll actually win it.

Street Justice

New Orleans is a charming city, but don't expect to find much of that charm when driving the streets. The guy who'll gladly share his throws from Endymion with anyone standing around him on the parade route is the same guy who'll abruptly cut people off in parade traffic on the way home.

Along with the few other sane drivers in this city, I had resigned myself to the fact that I would just have to learn to deal with the ill-mannered motorists out there and accept their shortcomings as part of the price of living here. I never even entertained the thought that I could be a vigilante.

But a little red Corvette in the parking lot of Lakeside Mall recently changed that. Parked in the very first row, the sassy convertible—with leather seats and four-on-the-floor—was hogging two primo spaces.

On the other hand, my minivan—with child-restraint seats and stale-Cheerios-on-the-floor—was parked a full light year away in the only spot I could find, a narrow squeeze between a couple of two-door coupes destined to "ding" my van while I shopped. As I walked toward the mall and passed the offending car, I found myself entertaining various revenge scenarios, everything from letting the air out of its tires to giving it a thorough machine-gunning. But in the end, I settled for scribbling the word *HOG* on a piece of paper and placing

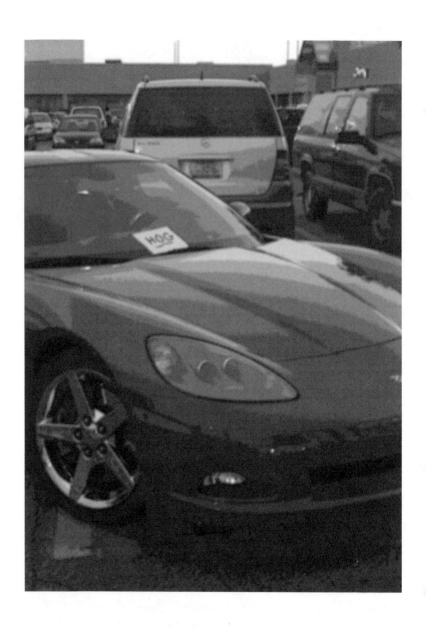

it under the windshield wiper on my way into Dillard's.

A small gesture, for sure, but nonetheless marvelously satisfying. No doubt hundreds of other shoppers had passed that car and shaken their heads, but *I* had done something about it. Would it change the 'Vette's owner into a more considerate human being? Probably not, but somehow it had changed me. I had had my say, and I liked the feeling.

As I drove off, I found myself anxiously awaiting another opportunity to dish out some small-scale justice, waiting for another inconsiderate jerk to "make my day." Unlike Mr. Eastwood, however, I couldn't pull out a six-shooter to dispense some frontier justice. Still, I figured there ought to be a way for us courteous drivers to deal with the morons who take advantage of the rest of us. But how?

And, lo, there on the passenger seat next to me was the answer. Perhaps Clint's gun was a little too extreme, but my son's paintball gun was perfect! At the next red light I picked it up. Yep, I was holding in my hands what could be—what should be—the instrument of a new justice system. Paintball justice.

Driving behind a slob who tosses an empty Barq's can onto Carrollton Avenue? Ka-pow! He won't even know what hit him. Being passed on the right by a moron driving on the shoulder of Earhart Expressway to get around all the other drivers patiently waiting in line? Ka-splat! And what about the idiot at the front of the line who lets him in? Save a shot for him too. Ka-plooey!

Drivers with three or more hits would be ticketed by New Orleans and Jefferson Parish police. Only then will authorities erase the phosphorescent orange ink with a special solvent. The offender now gets a fresh start and has a chance to move from "jerk" category to "decent human being" category.

As I drove home, I considered the educational component

of this system. Take, for example, the cute but clueless teenager in the car ahead of me yesterday at Whitney Bank's drive-up window. The two of us had been creeping forward in line for several minutes, until it was finally her turn at the window. Only then, however, did she begin an exhaustive search for a pen. She eventually found one under the seat, but—oops, she didn't have a deposit slip. (And the line next to mine—the line I almost chose—advanced another car.) After receiving a slip from the teller, she filled it out, sent in her check, and eventually got her cash. But instead of driving up one space to allow me to begin my transaction, she meticulously arranged the bills in her wallet and then searched for her sunglasses at the bottom of her purse. (Another car in the lucky line next to mine advanced.) She adjusted her radio, the rearview mirror, the AC, and her seatbelt. After reapplying lipstick, she finally drove off. If I'd had that paintball gun . . . Ka-pow! *There's* a life lesson they don't teach in high school.

As I pondered such scenarios and the heady satisfaction that paintball justice would bring, I reached my driveway— before meting out a single sentence. But parked in front of my neighbor's house was a lawn-maintenance truck. And inside it were the culprits who get rid of my neighbor's grass clippings by blowing them off his lawn—and onto mine. A worker emerged from the truck with a huge leaf-blower strapped to his back. He wrapped his fingers around the starter. My fingers found the trigger of the paintball gun. Our eyes met. "Go ahead," I whispered. "Make my day. . . . "

A Place in the Sun
Can Leave You Burned

Since New Orleans isn't actually on the Gulf of Mexico (yet), for decades the beach of choice has been the Mississippi coast for thousands of local families—including mine.

In 1953 my parents read an ad in the *Times-Picayune:* "Quaint summer cottage on the shores of a dreamy bayou. Within walking distance of the beautiful beaches of the Gulf of Mexico."

For this young couple, pregnant with their first—and most charming and intelligent—child, the enchanting description in the real-estate ads must have sounded good. With high hopes they made the trip from New Orleans to the tiny beach town of Pass Christian.

There they discovered the true meaning of the pretty words in the ad.

"Quaint summer cottage" more precisely translated to "Small, unpainted, clapboard camp with four tiny rooms—a miniature kitchen, a petite den, an undersized bedroom, and a claustrophobic bathroom."

"On the shores of" meant "Down in a gully at the far edge of a narrow lot."

The "dreamy bayou" was a stagnant drainage ditch along the rear line of the property.

"Within walking distance of the gulf" was technically correct— for anyone who regularly trained for cross-country marathons.

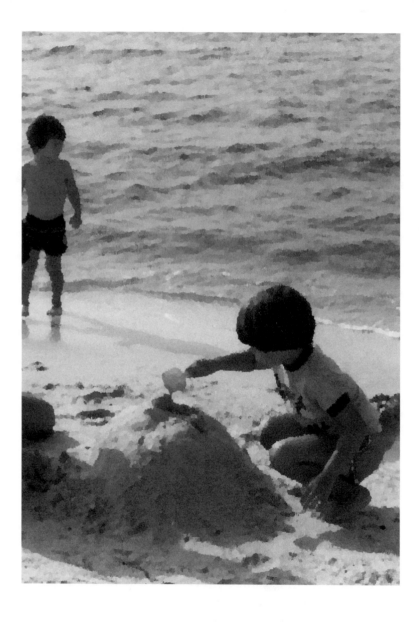

But the screened porch that surrounded three sides of the house sure looked inviting, and the long-needle pines that managed to root in the sandy, orange-clay soil swayed in an embracing breeze. Furthermore, the real-estate agent assured them that within the next few months the "bayou" at the rear of the property would be opened on the north end, allowing a nearby river to infuse the waterway with fresh, flowing water. The drainage ditch would soon become a picturesque, vibrant stream racing to the Gulf of Mexico and carrying with it a bounty of fresh fish and shrimp.

My parents wistfully imagined their sweet, little, as-yet unborn children joyfully romping and playing in the yard, fishing from the bayou, and drinking homemade lemonade on the porch.

So with dreamy optimism, they purchased the property, planning to add on to the house one day and counting on the agent's integrity about the coming changes to the bayou.

Decades later the four small rooms were still four small rooms, and the drainage ditch was still a drainage ditch.

And the sweet little children joyfully romping and playing in the yard never materialized.

Instead, they got us.

And what we looked forward to more than anything else was an afternoon at the beach.

Ah, sand! In the movies, it's the stuff that tropical isles are made of. But in reality, it's a quadrillion particles of granular irritation. Which makes it perfect for aggravating one's siblings. Which is why we enjoyed going to the beach.

Afternoons began idyllically. Mom and Dad, comfortably settled under an umbrella, watched their children romping through the waves, building multi-turreted sand castles, and taking turns burying each other in the sand.

But sibling cooperation, being the unnatural state that it is, was short-lived. The castles that lined the water's edge were destroyed one by one—not by the imminent encroachment of the tide but by something far more imminent—a sibling plot. Of course, none of the demolitions was intentional. Each was an unfortunate "accident."

Taking turns burying each other in the sand was innocent enough at first, but then the latent symbolism in the game began to emerge. The "graves" we dug for each other got deeper. The sand piled on top of the person was packed harder. And then the buriers would "accidentally" forget the buried and run off to play in the surf. The buried's cries were accidentally ignored.

Dad tried to turn things around by organizing games. In one attempt, he placed two empty pails on the beach, lined us up about twenty yards away, and gave each of the three-man teams a small plastic shovel. The object of the game was to carry small shovelfuls of sand to the team's bucket, and the first team to fill their bucket would win.

It worked well enough for a while. Then I noticed that the boys' team won every round. I began to watch my brother and noticed that after dumping his shovelful of sand into the bucket, he would shake his leg, and—lo and behold—an extra helping of sand would fall from his swimming trunks into the bucket.

I had discovered the ploy, but I said nothing, because I had also noticed that the contraband was beginning to exact its toll. That extra shovelful of sand he had stuffed down his pants was starting to find its way into cracks and crevices he never knew he had, and it was rubbing them raw. Soon the fun of the game became watching my brother struggle to cover the distance from the starting line to the bucket. His "dash" to the buckets became a pained run. Then the run became a walk, the walk a limp, the limp a cower. Finally, he announced, "I quit," and ran toward the gulf.

The rest of the group laughed, but the best part was about to come. He was counting on the rushing waves to wash the sand from his crevices, but what he forgot to consider was the saline content of those waves. As soon as his rear end hit the gulf, the tender skin that had been rubbed raw by the sand was washed over by stinging salt water. His yeows could be heard over the cries of the gulls.

Sand, surf, and siblings—always a magical combination for a memorable day at the Mississippi beach.

Big Easy Etiquette

*Our own maven of manners, Miss Emilie Peaust,
known to her loyal readers as Ms. Manners,
answers etiquette questions unique to
the New Orleans area.*

Dear Ms. Manners:

We have just moved to New Orleans and have been invited to our first crawfish boil. Is it true that our dinner will still be alive when we first arrive at the party? My wife insists she will not be able to eat anything she had previously met when it was alive.

Please fill us in.

Sincerely,
New to Boils

Dear Boils:

Your dinner will indeed be alive when you first get there. However, although Ms. Manners herself would not want to meet a cute little bunny before it is sacrificed for her dinner and served under *sauce piquante,* she seriously doubts that your wife will form any lasting emotional bonds with a sack of crustaceans.

Just to be on the safe side, however, I suggest that you and your wife do not look any live crawfish directly in the eyes. And lest you feel guilty as you begin peeling and eating, remember that by choosing this dinner of lowly mudbugs, you may have spared a cute little bunny from that ultimate *sauce-piquante* fate.

Sincerely,
Ms. Manners

Dear Ms. Manners:

When it comes to securing a ladder for our son at parade time, my husband believes in SEL (Someone Else's Ladder). Unlike the other fathers who arrive early to secure a spot and then guard the ladder, sometimes for hours, we arrive just a few minutes before the parade. My husband then makes conversation with one of the ladder dads who has an empty spot on the seat next to his child, and eventually asks if our son could join his. Amazingly, he's never been turned down. After the parade ends, he leaves the other guy to struggle with taking down the ladder and hauling it away.

If the guy with the ladder is a relative, my husband doesn't even bother making polite conversation. He just holds up little Eric and asks the adult standing behind the ladder seat, "Is there room for your adorable little nephew up there?"

He's even been known to put Eric in temporarily unoccupied ladders when the parents briefly leave to take their children to the bathroom. When they return, he begs forgiveness, saying he thought the ladder was abandoned, and asks if little Eric can stay. This ploy works just as well as the others.

I tell him that ladder-poaching is unethical, but he says if more parents would do this, we would need fewer ladders and there would be more room for everyone at the parade. What do you say?

Wondering Mom

Dear Wondering Mom:

Was your family at the corner of Eighth and St. Charles for Okeanos last year? If so, tell "adorable little Eric" I expect him to return the stuffed animal and the pink pearls he pilfered from my daughter while he was sitting next to her on top of the ladder.

Expecting a Reply ASAP,
Ms. Manners

Dear Ms. Manners:

What is the proper way to deal with a sloppy roast beef po-boy?

Parkway Patron

Dear Patron:

Indeed, an eight-napkin po-boy can be a difficult meal to eat delicately. Fortunately, if you've run out of napkins, Big Easy etiquette generally dictates that it is okay to lick dripping gravy off your hand(s). However, it is not polite to lap any gravy running down your arms, especially if it gets past your elbows, or if your arms happen to be especially hairy.

And although dripping gravy is undeniably your major dilemma, it is not the only one. You're likely to lose a significant portion of your sandwich with each bite, as roast beef, mayo, gravy, and the occasional errant tomato will squirt/drop out unless you somehow manage to squeeze closed the sides and back end of the sandwich. Trying to ride herd on the sloppy ingredients is a very difficult feat to perfect. If you keep the back closed, stuff squishes out of the sides, and vice versa.

So you have a difficult choice to make: do you let the insides fall out of the sandwich and onto the paper wrapper, or do you try to hold the sandwich edges closed and get exponentially more gravy on your hands? If you choose the former, you may indeed use your fingers to pick up the fallen ingredients from the paper wrapper and eat them one piece at a time. On the other hand (no pun intended), it is not proper—and, unfortunately, I have seen it done on more than one occasion—to gather up the four corners of the paper wrapper, forcing all the contents to the middle, and then slurp them up with a loud sucking noise.

If you choose the latter and try to hold the po-boy closed with your hands, well, you're right back in the middle of the dripping-gravy issue.

In the end, if you can't handle the gravy, order a ham and Swiss.

Delicately yours,
Ms. Manners

Dear Ms. Manners:

I can accept the fact that streetcars have the right of way, and I always make sure that the coast is clear before I make a left turn onto the neutral ground. However, sometimes the cross traffic is so heavy that I'm caught there for a while. Meanwhile, a streetcar that was six blocks away at the time I turned eventually gets to where I'm stuck. It pulls up to within inches of my passenger-side door and dings the bell incessantly, expecting me to somehow move out of the way. If I don't immediately rush headlong into oncoming traffic and perish in flames, the streetcar moves even closer and rings that bell louder and faster. I don't know what's worse: the flames or that damn bell.

Is it right for them to do this?

Must we put up with this unfair and infuriating behavior?

Streetcar Hater

Dear Streetcar Hater:

No.

Yes.

Ms. Manners

Dear Ms. Manners:

My bride and I visited your wonderful city on our honeymoon. We had a marvelous time, but we were quite confused by one of your local customs. People would tell us: "Let's say, 'Lay bunt on ruler.'" So, of course, we obliged their request and proceeded to say, "Lay bunt on ruler." They seemed real happy when we did this. Why do they keep asking us to say this? And what bunt are they talking about? Where is the ruler we were supposed to lay it down on?

We're worried we may have insulted local people by not following through correctly with this custom.

Curious Honeymooners

Dear Honeymooners:

Ah, *mes amis!* Put the ruler away and drop the bunt. The expression you heard is *"Laissez les bons temps rouler,"* French for "Let the good times roll." It's a philosophy the locals believe in. And if you were here on your honeymoon, I'm sure you correctly followed through with that philosophy on several occasions!

Ms. Manners

Dear Ms. Manners:

Several months ago my brother and I had a fight with our sister. I won't go into all the details, but it involves a lack of attendance of certain family members at a very long and boring dance recital for her fat, clumsy, wannabe-ballerina daughter.

The feud itself is not the problem. The problem is that my vengeful sister has rented an apartment on the parade route. I am convinced she did this purely out of spite.

Unbelievably, my brother plans to make up with Sis when parade season approaches, just so he can have a bathroom to use for him and his kids. I've told him that if he goes through with the reconciliation, he is ditching his self-respect, pride, and dignity in exchange for a toilet.

I, on the other hand, plan to stand my ground. What do you think?

Betrayed Brother

Dear Brother:

Pride and dignity can't hold a candle to a toilet on Mardi Gras day. Call me after your third beer and let me know how the apology went.

Ms. Manners

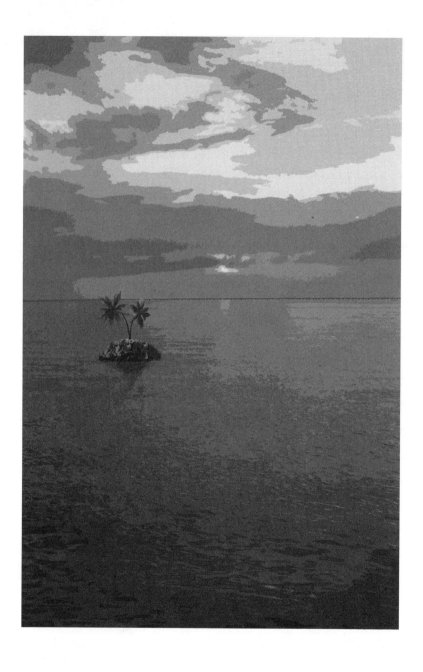

Isle Be There

By most accounts, Lake Pontchartrain is a nice enough lake. It's really big. It gives us bragging rights to the title "longest bridge in world." It has pretty sunrises on one side and pretty sunsets on the other. It's great for crabbing, fishing, and boating. And ask any teenager about the exciting submarine races to be found there.

But nice as it is, Lake Pontchartrain is seriously lacking in one respect: it doesn't have an island. Not even a decent atoll. It's an embarrassing shortcoming—a disappointment, even. Isolated islets of marshy muck along the shoreline notwithstanding, there ought to be a real, honest-to-goodness, totally-surrounded-by-water island stuck right in the middle of the lake.

Fortunately, the fact that there is no natural island does not preclude us from producing an "unnatural" one. In fact, back in the 1920s a group of businessmen purportedly suggested a similar idea. They proposed that a string of small, artificial islands be constructed in hopscotch fashion across the lake with bridges interlinking the islands and connecting them to both shores. This newly born real estate was to be sold to wealthy citizens, who would then build stately homes on the isles. Proceeds from the sales and subsequent property taxes would help finance the construction of the project. The series of interisland bridges would deliver travelers from one shore to the other. Not a bad idea, except that it didn't get beyond the proposal stage. The islands never happened.

And now, almost a century later, we've got the Causeway and the Twin Spans to carry us across, so we don't need five or six islets. What we need is one, solid, not-so-measly island. Perfectly doable. After all, if Dubai can build an entire archipelago in the Persian Gulf, certainly we can build one good island in the middle of Lake Pontchartrain.

Although a plain old round island would serve just fine, why not go hog wild and build the island in the shape of a giant fleur de lis? Or how about one in the shape of a saxophone—or a trumpet? Nothing wrong with a humongous crescent, either.

Whatever the shape, the next step will be to come up with a good mixture to use for fill—and we won't have to look far for ingredients. Begin by collecting the mountains of discarded oyster shells from Drago's, Acme, Felix's, and Casamento's. Supplement with mussel shells from La Crepe Nanou and crab shells from Middendorf's.

Next, mix in the tons of trash left behind after Mardi Gras parades: broken beads, empty beer bottles, and discarded Popeye's chicken bones—all the debris collected by those annoying sweeper trucks that follow so closely behind the last float that you barely have time to pry Grandma from her lawn chair before she disappears between the ravenous rotating sweeper brushes in a blast of water and is sucked beneath the truck.

Crush and add in the unclaimed ladders and abandoned sofas that litter the neutral ground on Ash Wednesday morning.

Scoop up all the loose asphalt from the crumbling streets in Lakeview and dump it in.

Collect all the shoes and sandals left stuck in the mud after Jazz Fest and throw them in.

If necessary, supplement with wadded-up *Times-Picayune* newspapers. If it's good enough for the Army Corps of Engineers to use in the expansion joints of floodwalls, then it's good enough to use in the building of our island.

Mix the ingredients well, adding just enough concrete to bind it all together. Then start pumping it all in. Before you know it, we'll have a genuine island rising up through the surface of the water. Land ho!

For aesthetics, finish off the surface of the island with a fertile layer of topsoil. How about a mixture of spillway sand laced with a year's worth of used coffee grinds donated by Café Du Monde, Morning Call, PJ's, and CC's? Then bind it all together with truckloads of droppings donated by the Fair Grounds' racehorses. After it airs out a little, we'll have a super-fertilized layer of earth, primed and ready to grow.

Voila, mes amis! An island!

Then it's all ready for, for . . .

Ah, the possibilities boggle the mind! We could return to the original 1920s idea and let the rich guys have it. Sell it off to the well-to-do to build stately mansions and ritzy hotels—sort of a St. Charles Avenue on the lake, or rather, in the lake. Then again, if we've got only one island, should we really let just the privileged few enjoy it?

Nah. Instead of mansions, how about recreating the camps that used to line the lake's shores in Little Woods, Irish Bayou, and North Shore beach? To make the re-creation authentic, the camps should come complete with screen doors that squeak, long rickety fishing piers that jut out into the lake, and screened-in porches that are just right for eating boiled crabs and playing bourré long into the night by the light of yellow, mosquito-repelling light bulbs. Heaven on earth! Rent the camps out to local families and tourists.

Then again, wouldn't the island be the perfect place for a grand amusement park? First, pave a wide asphalt midway right down the middle of the island. Flank it with a penny arcade on one side and a performance stage on the other. Next, add a Zephyr, Wild Maus, Laff in the Dark, Kiddie Land, bumper cars, and Ferris wheel. Include a tiki-type restaurant at one end and a lighthouse near the entrance. Don't forget a large swimming pool with a stomach-churning hell dive. Dump spillway sand behind the stage and you've got a real beach for swimming. Now *that's* an amusement park.

Or make it a food and music Mecca. Imagine a 24/7/365 Jazz Fest—without the Gentilly parking hassles. Boats ferry fest-goers from large parking lots on either shore. Live bands perform on giant outdoor stages—the best of gospel, rock, jazz, pop, zydeco, and R&B—all day, all year. Plant a big flagpole right in the middle so friends know where to meet. The top restaurants in the city can offer renowned favorites from booths scattered all over the island. In addition, Fitzgerald's, Bruning's, and the other restaurants that used to line West End Park, even the My-Oh-My Club, can reopen along its shores—all on pilings over the water, of course.

And best of all, it's "pay one price." Once you hit the shore of Festival Island, you can listen to all the Irma Thomas, eat all the crawfish Monica, and drink all the Sazeracs you can possibly handle.

Then again, maybe we should do a big 180 and think less happy thoughts for the island. Perhaps we should use it for a Big Easy version of Alcatraz—an isolated, escape-proof prison reserved for the worst kinds of criminals—such as politicians who bamboozle citizens, sleazy contractors who prey upon little old ladies, and oil-company execs who put the bottom line ahead of all else. If there's any room left, throw in a few chefs who've been caught using Chinese crawfish, a handful of overzealous CBD meter maids, and jerks who cut in front of the first row at parades and stand in front of small children. Make the prison inescapable by surrounding it with a gator-infested moat.

With so many good possibilities for this soon-to-be island, it's going to be tough to choose only one. Which brings us back to the original 1920s proposal. Perhaps they had it right all along. We're definitely going to need more than one island.

Everything I Needed to Know in Life I Learned at a Crawfish Boil

The cold, cruel world can be a tough teacher. Fortunately, life's lessons can be just as well learned—and much easier to digest—at a crawfish boil. There's more going on than just pinching tails and sucking heads. There are important principles to be learned:

~~~~~~~~~~~~

On the culinary ladder of life, it's better to be on the "eatin'" end instead of the "eaten" end. The creatures on the table got there because they went after an easy meal of chicken necks tied to nets dropped right in front of them. If any one of those hundreds of recently deceased and soon-to-be-consumed crawfish on the table were to be given a second chance, he would surely have some sage advice:

⚜ *Beware of the easy bait the world dangles in front of you.* ⚜

If something looks too good to be true—and you go for it anyway—you could end up getting your tail burned.

~~~~~~~~~~~~

It's not the actual boiling that makes the crustacean taste so good; it's the simmering and soaking afterward that transform the "beast" to "feast." There's nothing like the disappointing taste of bland crawfish served by an overeager host to remind us that:

❧ *The good things in life are worth waiting for.* ❧

People who look for shortcuts and instant gratification in this world are likely to be sorely disappointed. On the other hand, consistency and patience will not only get you an unfailingly good batch of spicy, steaming crawfish, it could also get you where you want to go in life.

~~~~~~~~~~~

For every dozen people sitting at the table eating, there's one guy slaving over a steaming boiler, knowing he's going to be the last one to eat. He's also the most appreciated person there and the most likely to be invited as a guest to the next party. He knows it's important to:

❧ *Give of yourself.* ❧

You can't always be on the receiving end of everything, and if you try, you'll find yourself without friends. Besides, it gives you a warm, fuzzy feeling to take your turn as cook.

~~~~~~~~~~~

Behold the lowly mudbug—a most unappealing creature

who lives in a swampy hole in the ground. Yet with the right preparation, he attains the loftiest heights of culinary appeal, proof positive that:

⚜ *Appearances can be deceiving.* ⚜

Some of life's moments can be dreadfully ugly, too—moments that at the time seem to promise nothing good. But season them with a positive attitude and let them simmer in the passage of time. Chances are you'll look back one day to find that these ugly moments—while closing an easy door—had opened an unexpected window that led to a better road.

~~~~~~~~~~~

It's a beautiful Sunday afternoon and there are a dozen people sitting around makeshift tables in your backyard growing increasingly tantalized by the smell of that first batch of crawfish a-boiling away. They're talking and laughing over the roar of the flame under the pot, when all of a sudden there's a sputtering—and then cold silence. You've run out of propane. If you don't have a spare tank on hand, the party will grind to a halt. Any Boy Scout could have told you to:

⚜ *Be prepared.* ⚜

Life is going to throw you curveballs, too. You can't anticipate everything, but you'll save yourself a lot of grief if you take the time to check the propane in your tank before you start.

~~~~~~~~~~~

Peeling crawfish is a messy proposition. The "juice" runs down your arms, yellow head fat stains your clothes, and the smell just won't wash off your fingers. But those delicious crawfish on the table in front of you are not going to peel themselves. The messy truth is:

⚜ *Sometimes you gotta get your hands dirty.* ⚜

The finer things in life rarely come served on a silver platter either. So, roll up your sleeves. Otherwise, you might miss out on the good stuff.

~~~~~~~~~~~

Some like it hot; some tend to go easy on the cayenne. No matter what spice proportion you use, some of your guests will think the crawfish are underseasoned; some overseasoned. Too much salt; not enough. Way too much garlic; not enough corn. Face it:

⚜ *You can't please everybody.* ⚜

Despite their individual judgments on the seasoning, you can bet that none of your guests will pass up the feast in front of them.

It's the nature of the world that people are going to pull you in opposite directions—some demanding you do things one way, others demanding just the opposite. Trust your instincts. Call it the way you see it, go for a happy medium, and then don't let the complaints get to you.

~~~~~~~~~~~

Some boiled crawfish are just too spicy to swallow. Others may have no taste at all. Then again, every once in a while you'll pick up a "straight tail" and wish you hadn't taken the chance. The best you can do is:

⚜ *Learn to take the bad with the good.* ⚜

Some of life's days are unbearable, some humdrum, some rotten. But most of them are pretty darned good if you try to make the most of each one that comes your way.

~~~~~~~~~~~~

People who look on in disgust at those who suck the heads may not know what they're missing. If only they would gather up the courage to:

⚜ *Be adventurous.* ⚜

When you think you've got this world by the tail, don't be afraid to shake things up a little and try something new, do something daring, seek something uncommon.

~~~~~~~~~~~~

Somehow, boiled crawfish always taste better when you enjoy them with friends. So, be sure to:

⚜ *Share.* ⚜

Moments and memories are sweeter when you're surrounded by those you love.

~ ~ ~ ~ ~ ~ ~ ~ ~ ~ ~

And:

❧ *Family is even more important than friends.* ❧

When the cold beer of life runs out, it's family that hangs around longer.

~ ~ ~ ~ ~ ~ ~ ~ ~ ~ ~

Friends. Family. Food. Fun. Find your place at the table and:

❧ *Laissez les bons temps rouler!* ❧

Swamp Safari

The representative from Southeast Louisiana Swamp District 1 stood in the doorway, welcoming his constituents. "Come on in," he beckoned. "There's plenty of room. Moms, please drop off the little ones at our youth session in the annex. They can join us later. We've got some important issues to attend to first."

When the crowd had settled in their seats, the councilman—known to all as Big Jake—slowly made his way to the dais, smoothing back his dark brown hair along the way and greeting the citizens as he passed. "I hereby call this meeting to order," Big Jake said with a rap of the gavel. He was taller than most in the room, but it was his clear, resonant voice that gave him the air of authority.

"I'd like to begin this assembly with a moment of remembrance for four of our neighbors who died tragically this week. Let us always hold in our hearts the memory of Mark and Evelyn—both shot to death in cold blood; Frank—hauled away by bounty hunters; and, saddest of all, young Derrick—eaten alive by that cursèd gator, Big Bessie." A hushed, reverent silence fell, and the members of the group bowed their heads. After several seconds the representative gave the signal, and everyone in the room thumped their tails on the floor. Once. Then again. Then

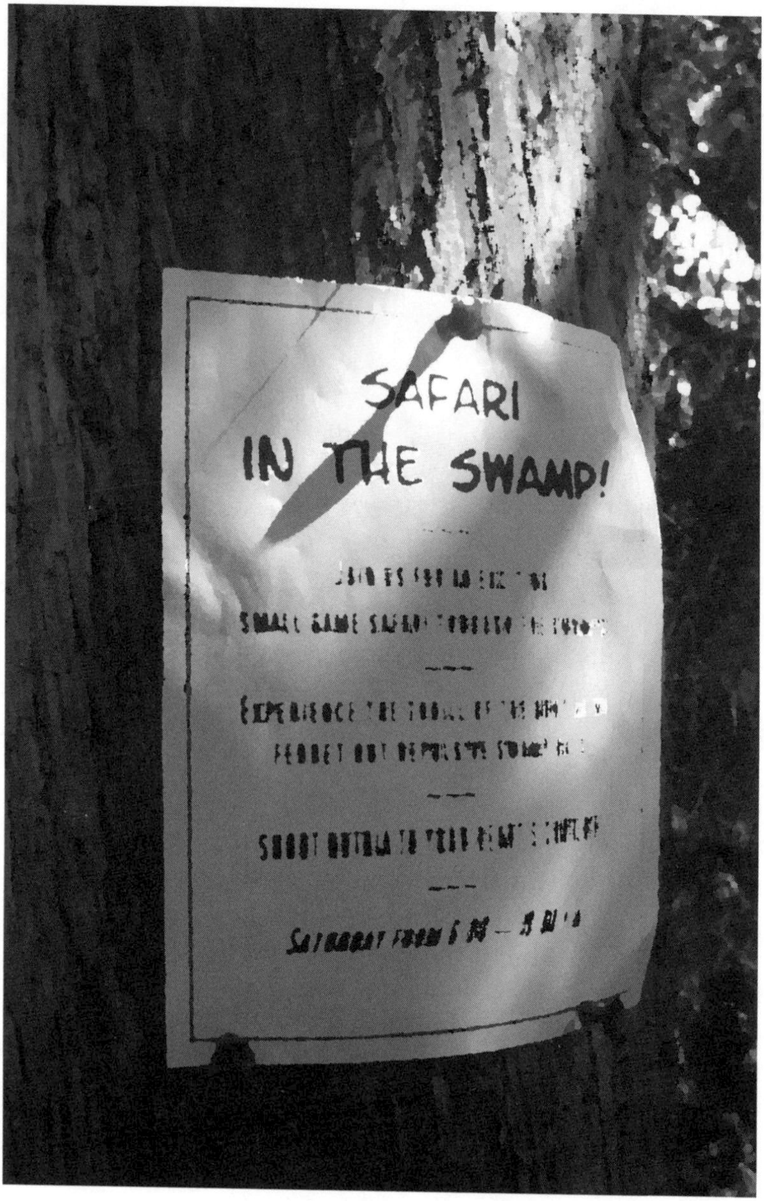
SAFARI
IN THE SWAMP!

two more times. One somber thump for each of their newly deceased neighbors.

"Thank you, ladies and gentlemen," said Big Jake. Then he flashed a big, orange, toothy grin like the practiced politician that he was. Reelected three times, he looked out at the several hundred nutria gathered before him who, time and again, had turned to him for leadership.

"We have plenty to cover tonight, my friends, so let's get right to the committee reports," said Big Jake. "We'll start with Finance."

The heavyset treasurer, known as Moose, stood to present his report. As the room waited in silence, he gave his left whiskers a twist, then his right. Slowly and with a husky voice, he finally began, "Things are looking good in this department, Big Jake. Our long-standing contract with the old trapper T-Bob has definitely worked to our advantage. As you know, we now have 100 percent participation from the District 1 community in the donor program, whereby every citizen has agreed to donate his tail upon natural death. We deliver all the donor tails to T-Bob, who collects the five-dollar tail bounty from the state, takes his 20 percent, and gives the balance to us."

"Hold on, Moose," interrupted Big Jake. "Are we absolutely sure T-Bob isn't killing any of our citizens himself and collecting tail bounties on the victims?"

Moose looked around at his group of henchmen, gave a knowing, carrot-colored smile, and replied, "Absolutely sure, Big Jake. According to the contract, he can't even launch his pirogue into the swamp. Me and my boys here keep a real close eye on him. He tried it a couple of years ago, and we chewed a hole in the bottom of his boat before he could even pull away from the dock. T-Bob learned his lesson. Besides, he's fat and happy with his 20 percent. Got enough to keep his fridge full of beer, and that's all he really cares about." A snicker reverberated through the room at T-Bob's expense.

"We're sitting pretty ourselves," Moose continued, his hefty jowls jiggling as he spoke. "Plenty in the coffers to buy us another couple of people in Baton Rouge—if you get my drift." Then with a satisfied smile on his face, the corpulent coypu sat down.

"Good work, Moose," said Big Jake. "Public Relations, would you go next?"

"Sure thing, Big Jake," answered Miss Melanie with a sugar-sweet and exaggerated Southern drawl. Small statured and still in possession of her trim girlish figure, Melanie clambered up onto her chair so the audience could see her better. Balancing deftly on her hindquarters, she held up a colorful poster with her two front paws—an action that quite coincidentally showed off her newly manicured, candy-apple-red claws. "As you know, our committee is working to improve the public's perception of our image. Hence this poster, which will soon appear all over South Louisiana. As you can see, we have a very attractive model here, orange teeth toned down a notch and tail hidden behind some strategically placed palmetto bushes."

"Hey," interrupted Mrs. Gloria, "that's you. You're the model!"

Miss Melanie stopped and turned toward Mrs. Gloria seated on the third row. "Yes, Mrs. Gloria. It is I in the poster," answered Melanie in a tone that was just a wee bit patronizing. Melanie knew that Gloria—who had lost her youth and girlish figure long ago—was probably a tad jealous, so she didn't take umbrage at the interruption. "I posed for free," she continued, "to save us the money we would have had to pay for a professional coypu model." After an almost imperceptible impatient twitching of her whiskers at Gloria, Melanie turned back to the audience. "The goal of this campaign is to have human people see us in a better light—less repulsive and more 'adorable,' if you will—more like swamp beavers than swamp rats. Our polls tell us that humans perceive beavers to be considerably cuter and much less abhorrent than rats. Thus, you will note the little twig dam in the background—for a stronger subliminal association with beavers."

"So, why is this fixation on image so important?" interrupted Mrs. Gloria again rudely, oblivious to the fact that her own image was suffering due to her protests. Mrs. Gloria was only bringing attention to the glaring differences between the brusque demeanor of the matronly icon and the sweet nature of the perfectly airbrushed Melanie.

"People are a lot less likely to spend time and money on eradication plans if they think of us as cute and harmless, rather than ugly and threatening," Melanie said, addressing the entire assembly.

The audience members nodded, and Miss Melanie proceeded to climb down from her chair, a provocative feat monitored closely by the male attendees, who followed every movement of her curvaceous hindquarters. Then, with a coquettish swish of her tail, she took her seat.

"Thank you so very much, Miss Melanie," Big Jake cooed. Then after clearing his throat and regaining his professional composure, he said, "Let's go to old business next—specifically Big Bessie. We have to do something with that damned gator, or we'll keep losing our little ones. It's appalling. I see your paw up, Don. Let's hear your suggestion."

With a squirrely demeanor, Don hopped up onto his chair in one swift motion. He was as hyper as nutria come. "I propose we take some of our cash from the tail bounties and offer a big reward to the human trappers. Let them do our dirty work for us and get rid of Big Bessie." There was a general murmur of agreement from the audience. Don continued, "I already talked to Justin, our contact in da parish, and he's agreed to set it all up—as long as we cut him in with a portion of the reward when Big Bessie's caught."

"Seconded!" shouted someone from the back of the room.

"Passed," stated Big Jake with a rap of his gavel. "On to new business," he said next. "Anyone have something to bring up?"

"I do," said J.T. He stood at his place and waved a bright yellow flier. "Look at this, Big Jake. We found these all around da parish. 'Safari in the Swamp!' it says." The audience murmured in alarm. J.T. continued reading aloud: "'Join us for an exciting small-game safari through the swamps. Experience the thrill of the hunt as we ferret out repulsive swamp rats. Shoot nutria to your heart's content. Saturday from 6:00 to 10:00 p.m.'" Unable to contain his anger, J.T. ripped up the flier and sent confetti-like pieces sailing into the audience. "We have to do something about this, Big Jake!" he cried. Clamor from the terrified citizens backed up his demand.

"Calm down, folks," said Big Jake, rearing up on his

hindquarters to speak over the noise of the audience. "It's a lot simpler than you think. Besides, we don't have time to come up with a complex plan. All we need to do is lie low on Saturday. These guys will be looking for swimming prey. So burrow in deep from 6:00 to 10:00. Keep real close tabs on the kids. We'll all be fine. I promise."

Big Jake gave the audience a minute to calm down; then he deftly switched gears. "How about some entertainment, folks? This week we've got a treat from the kids. Sophie, will you bring the little ones in?"

Sighs of "awww" emanated from the audience as three dozen adorable little nutria filed into the room. Some were shy and held their paws up in front of their faces—which made them all the cuter. Others confidently strode into the room, anxious to be the center of attention. Once Miss Sophie got them all lined up on the risers on the stage, she faced her pupils with her back to the audience and raised her paws, signaling for their quiet attention. The young group immediately quieted down. Miss Sophie had always had a way with the little ones.

Then she turned to address the audience. "Okay, Moms and Dads, we've been practicing this for weeks and we are all so excited to bring our performance to you. I'm sure you'll all recognize the tune: 'Do You Know What It Means to Miss New Orleans?' Well, we'd like to present you with our very own version." She turned her back to the audience, faced her pupils, and raised her baton. Miss Sophie moved her baton in time to the music, her tail and hindquarters swinging to the tune also. The little coypu took a deep breath and began. Slowly, and with paw motions to accompany the lyrics, the children sang from the heart:

Do you know what it means
To munch New Orleans,
To munch levees night and day?
It's here we belong;
Our number's getting stronger;
We're home and we plan to stay!

Then while the children continued a quiet humming of the melody, Miss Sophie turned to the audience and invited them to join the children in song. Overcome with sentiment and pride, everyone stood up to sing. The children repeated the verse as the audience joined in, and the room fairly swayed with heartfelt emotion.

Wild applause broke out after the performance. The children took a bow and smiled broadly, showing bright-orange teeth in the middle of their little white muzzles. Giggling with excitement, they exited the stage.

Big Jake returned to the dais while the buzz was still coursing through the audience and waited while the little coypu ran to find their parents in the crowd. He had to speak loudly to be heard over the commotion. "Congratulations, children!" he said. "And thank you, Miss Sophie. That was wonderful!

"Okay. As usual, we have a community meal prepared for all of you. Join us in the dining hall for a salad of cordgrass, spikerushes, and cattails. As a special treat we have soufflé of bald cypress bark. And save room for dessert: sugarcane!"

Big Jake was delighted with the change in atmosphere from the abject fear sparked by the safari flier just a few minutes ago. He gazed out at the nutria community—his nutria community—who had looked to him for leadership in the best of times and the worst of times. Although he, too, was anxious about the safari, he knew that every one of his constituents would be okay if they were careful and watched out for each other, just like the real community that they were. How proud he was of each and every one of the voters in front of him!

Big Jake beamed broadly, his tail swaying in contentment, as he stepped down from the stage to join the others at the buffet tables.

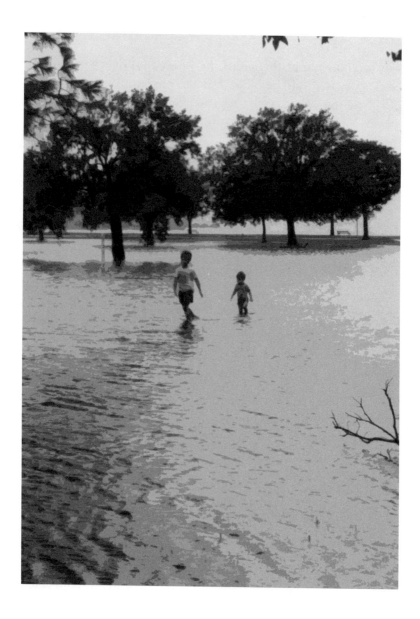

Grime and Punishment

Is it my imagination, or do New Orleans children tolerate dirt much better than their counterparts elsewhere do? Perhaps their laissez-faire attitude toward grime has evolved from the dozens of parades they have attended where they think nothing of sifting through gutter debris to retrieve a doubloon and then using those same grubby little fingers to stuff cotton candy in their mouths before licking their fingers clean. Perhaps it evolved from rolling down muddy levees. Or sloshing through knee-high waters from May floods. Or skim-boarding over seas of muck in City Park after near-miss hurricanes. In any case, New Orleans children have been conditioned to associate dirt with fun.

Perhaps this subconscious correlation explains my young yat's aversion to cleanliness. To hear him tell it, washing his hands before meals is a meaningless ritual intended only to prolong his hunger. Using a tissue to blow his nose is an unconscionable waste of paper, especially if a sleeve is readily available. But taking a shower is the most absurd practice of all—an unwarranted squandering of time and water, especially since he will be getting dirty again the next day. To him, "Grandma Beads," the little black rings of sweat-congealed dirt that accumulate in the folds of his neck, signify to all that he has spent a good day having fun. Why would we want to take this badge of honor away from him?

Over the years we have tried to convince him of the advantages of a daily de-griming. But almost without exception, the logic has backfired. My husband once detailed for him the awful things that happened to a little boy from Lakeview who didn't take a bath or wash his hair for an entire month. Crust formed in his armpits. Mushrooms began to grow in the grime between his toes. Roaches took up residence in his matted hair. My son's eyes lit up at the prospect. "Cool!" he said.

So each night, when he is sentenced to the cruel and unusual punishment of a shower, the combat commences. The routine includes a tedious repertoire of whining protests followed by a well-rehearsed series of delaying tactics. Night after night after night.

Until tonight. To my utter surprise, he complied with my "bath time!" decree without so much as a whimper, skipping off to the bathroom with a grin on his face. I stood aghast when I heard the water running. Had it really been that easy? Were the exhausting nightly battles soon to be a thing of the past? Had I just witnessed the slightest sliver of a ray of hope that he was entering a new, more mature, more hygienic phase?

I had the answer a mere three minutes later, when, dressed in pajamas, he emerged from the bathroom and sauntered past me. One whiff was enough to confirm that he remained unscathed by water.

With the buttons of his pajama top askew and his pajama pants inside out, he strode through the den toward a spot on the sofa, apparently confident that the threat of true cleanliness had passed.

Careful not to use an accusatory tone, I asked him

oh-so-nonchalantly if he had indeed taken a shower.

Already adept at slinging red herrings, he turned to me, feigning patience for my obvious lack of perception, and asked, "Didn't you hear the water running?"

I scowled. "Son, your hair isn't even wet. Get back in there and take a proper shower."

Grumbling, he stomped back toward the bathroom. This time the door slammed behind him. Again the water ran. A minute later he emerged and again walked confidently into the room. This time his hair was indeed wet, but his buttons were still askew and his pants still inside out. A seasoned pro, he then chose a seat on the other side of the room from me, downwind from the air-conditioning vent.

I eyed him suspiciously. "Sweetheart, you didn't just stick your head under the faucet to get your hair wet, did you?"

It wasn't the content of his answer but the delivery that was so impressive. Without taking his eyes from the television, he shook his head slowly and replied, "Aw, come *on,* Mom!" This was obviously a child who had just had his intentions maliciously maligned, his sincerity questioned, his character dragged through the dirt—literally.

But years of this game had left me a seasoned pro, also. I made an almost noiseless sniff of the air. And I knew that, like a hunted animal with heightened senses, he had heard the sniff. Yet he showed no reaction. Instead, he sat there watching television and pretended to be clean. So far it had taken him thirty minutes to try to get around what would have taken only ten minutes if he had done it right the first time. I sniffed again, this time a little louder. He was working hard to maintain his posture of innocence, but I saw him stiffen. He knew what was coming.

122

YAT WIT

"Come here, sweetie," I said gently. "Let me smell you."

His shoulders immediately sagged. The triumphant look drained from his face. Years of avoiding soap, shampoo, and toothpaste had taught him that a mother's most dangerous tool is her sense of smell. During the evolutionary process, it had grown more and more acute, because every mother in every generation has probably had a child like my son.

He walked slowly toward me and held out the backs of his hands for me to smell. But we had been down this road before. The dry white smear on his skin told me that he had rubbed the bar of soap across his hands, precisely for the "let-me-smell-you" scenario. It had worked only once.

"No, dear, turn around. I want to smell the back of your neck."

"But Mom . . . " he started, then broke off. He was busted and he knew it.

One quick sniff and I had the evidence I needed. It was time for the clincher, the one threat I had been saving for the occasion when nothing else had worked.

I turned him to face me, took a deep breath, pressed my lips together, and then slowly growled, "If you don't get in there and take a proper shower right this second, I will personally accompany you into the bathroom and scrub every inch of your body myself!"

He drew in a horrified gasp. A bright pink blush rose to his grimy little cheeks as he instinctively tried to cover his fully dressed body with his hands. "You wouldn't!" he cried.

I raised one eyebrow and met his stare. "Try me."

He jumped back out of my reach, then turned and ran to the bathroom.

This time the shower would be for real.

For a moment, I basked in my victory—the victory of cleanliness over filthiness, of wisdom over unreasonableness, of experienced adult over impetuous youth.

But I knew that my victory would be short-lived, for tomorrow he would be coming with us to Jazz Fest, where he will no doubt delight in slogging through six inches of muck on fairgrounds saturated by two days of rain.

So I knew better than to bask too long. Tomorrow night's bath time was only twenty-three and a half hours away.

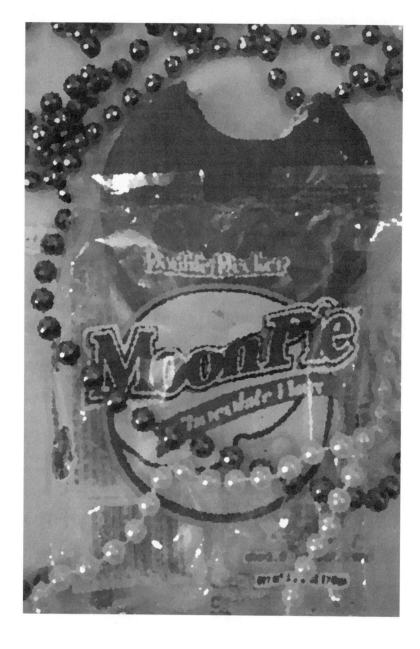

A Dozen Mardi Gras Lies That New Orleans Parents Tell Their Children

Wait, wait! The parade will be here any minute now. Stay up in the ladder!

The float rider threw this right to you. I just caught it for you when you weren't looking.

I'm sure we'll get just as many throws even if we didn't have time to make costumes this year.

What crumbs on my chin? No, of *course* I didn't eat that MoonPie you caught off the last float. I had to throw the whole thing away because the wrapper was torn and I didn't want you to get sick if you ate it.

I'd *love* to buy you some more Snap 'n' Pops, but unfortunately I've run out of money.

I'm *positive* it's okay to park here for the parade. So, stop worrying; we won't get a ticket.

Why buy a spear from that guy with the cart? I'm sure you'll catch one off a float today.

I did *not* put the baby in your slice of kingcake on purpose so that you would get it. You just happened to pick the right piece.

❧

That's the best shoebox Mardi Gras float I've ever seen!

❧

I don't want to miss Mardi Gras either, but this is the only week in the whole winter that the ski slopes are open.

❧

Getting the kingcake baby doesn't *really* mean you have to buy the next one for the entire class.

No, unfortunately, there aren't any parades tonight. So go ahead and start your homework.

Soufflé Sojourn

My Creole bread-pudding soufflé with warm whiskey cream from Commander's Palace is missing. As anyone in this city—and a goodly portion of the rest of the world—can tell you, bread-pudding soufflé is a wonderful thing. Indeed, it has powers all its own. Just thinking about it makes one smile. Tasting it is heaven. Warm, sweet, and satisfying, it is bread-pudding nirvana, capable of lifting one's spirits. The hint of whiskey in the sauce has strength sufficient to renew one's soul. Yet wonderful and powerful as it is, my bread pudding is AWOL.

Do not think that anything less than the greatest of care was taken with a parcel so prized. Transported home in its artistically crafted, aluminum-foil, swan-shaped "doggy bag," it was then camouflaged in a nondescript, brown-paper-bag overwrap. After much deliberation as to its safe storage, I quietly placed it behind the celery and broccoli in a bleak, uncharted region far back in my refrigerator. Just knowing it was there brought me joy for the rest of the day. I watched my daughter's soccer game in a thirty-degree drizzle, but—ah—I knew that my re-warmed bread pudding would be there for me later that night. My mud-caked son brought home three of his mud-caked friends, all of whom had spent the afternoon digging a tunnel under my back fence and into my neighbor's prized azaleas. But my bread pudding called to me from the refrigerator, and I felt comfort and solace.

Now, however, my treasure has vanished. Although I am not yet ready to give up the search, I must accept the fact that it has likely fallen victim to the unnatural, otherworldly, and inexplicable forces that govern my kitchen. It would not be the first time something bizarre happened in this puzzling region of my house. In fact, the disappearing dessert is just one more enigma in a long line of mysteries. Consider, for example, the paradox of why the garbage can in my kitchen is always overflowing.

Fortunately, I was eventually able to figure this one out, but first I had to get over that nonsense I learned in my science classes at Tulane about volume and critical mass. Instead, my children showed me the real truth—the truth that no matter how full the garbage can appears to be, you can always fit one more item on top. It's nothing short of miraculous how they can balance an empty peanut butter jar on top of an empty Krispy Kreme box, which is teetering on an empty two-liter bottle of Barq's, which is resting on a sea of slimy, leftover oatmeal. The reward? As long as they can fit one more item on top, the can isn't technically "full," so they don't have to take the bag to the trash outside and put in a new bag. Mystery solved.

At one time, I had also struggled with the conundrum of why the Bunny bread bag is never closed. For years I assumed it was pure laziness on the part of the person who had last removed a slice of bread. But what I have come to realize is that, while my family may be innately talented at balancing garbage, they are totally inept at closing twist ties. Although opening the tie doesn't pose a problem, some strange genetic defect has rendered their hands physically incapable of twisting it closed. Amazing stuff, especially if you've ever watched the deftness of those impaired little fingers when they're working a video game controller.

And for the longest time, I couldn't understand why there were always crumbs on the kitchen counter and sticky spots on the floor—no matter how often I cleaned. When I finally figured this one out, I was stunned by its profound implications: my children are trying to save our planet. The pieces came together when I saw a frightening documentary about the earth eventually meeting its doom from a catastrophic meteor hit. Within months, all life on the planet would cease to exist. Except for cockroaches. So all along my children have just been doing their part to nurture this hardy species to ensure that life on earth will endure—if even on the lowest level. Now that I look back, I am ashamed to think of all the times I squashed one of those disgusting, repulsive, disease-carrying little vermin, when the very future of our planet is at stake.

Like others before me, I've also wondered why children (and some husbands) stand in front of a refrigerator staring at the contents for extended periods of time when it actually takes only a few seconds to see what's inside.

Unlike the others, however, I have been able to solve this long-standing riddle. You see, refrigerators are apparently not the cold, lifeless, metal boxes we assume them to be. Rather, they are portals to an exciting, alternate universe—a universe where every imaginable junk food awaits. And the little light that goes on when you open the door is actually a powerful beacon, capable of beaming goodies over from the other side. The common belief among children (and some husbands) is that if they stare at the contents long enough while bathed in this supernatural light, better snacks and leftovers from the "other" side will miraculously appear through the transporter beam. Cool, huh?

But back to my missing Creole bread-pudding soufflé with warm whiskey cream. Despite my success at solving the other riddles, I am still stuck with the heartbreaking paradox of my lost pudding. You see, it's not the first time something like this has happened. Occasionally, instead of eating dessert with the rest of the family, I've announced that I'm saving mine to enjoy later after baths and bedtimes. Amazingly enough, the dessert sometimes disappears from the refrigerator before I can get to it. Just as my bread pudding did. Of course, it's never my husband or my children who take it. (I know because I've asked them.)

So I've begun to suspect that the long-held scientific principle about matter being neither created nor destroyed is pure hogwash. For, apparently, bread pudding—matter that it was—was destroyed. Poof!

But another explanation now occurs to me. Perhaps somewhere in an alternate universe there is another being—human or otherwise—who, at the end of a long day, was standing there in the enchanted transporter-beam light of the refrigerator the way her kids had taught her, when—presto—Creole bread-pudding soufflé with warm whiskey cream magically appeared!

Gee, I sure hope she took the time to enjoy a cup of café au lait with my bread pudding.

You Know You're in New Orleans If . . .

You know you're in New Orleans if . . .
the Tin Man is directing traffic around a fender bender while
a nun dressed as a convict and a convict dressed as a nun
exchange insurance information.

You know you're in New Orleans if . . .
you've ever said, "My house has been gutted four feet down!"
and then smiled broadly, because you know the other person
knew that this was a good thing, too.

You know you're in New Orleans if . . .
someone throws you a pair of underwear from the back of a
truck and you cheer and put them on your head.

You know you're in New Orleans if . . .
you've ever told your child not to eat the "dead man's fingers"
and your child said, "Yeah, I know, Dad."

You know you're in New Orleans if . . .
you don't cringe when someone mentions that his uncle
Oil will be fryin' swimps in berling erl on the banquette
by Ly-ola.

You know you're in New Orleans if . . .
you and six of your closest friends frantically scream out the name of a man you have never met just because one of them knows someone who knows someone who has a cousin riding on the neutral-ground side of a truck travelling down a major thoroughfare.

You know you're in New Orleans if . . .
a man you have never met pelts you and six of your closest friends with beads just because there's a chance that he knows someone who knows someone who has a cousin in your group.

You know you're in New Orleans if . . .
you get that fingernails-scraping-across-a-blackboard feeling upon hearing the pronunciations "pray-leenz," "pee-cans," or "cray-fish."

You know you're in New Orleans if . . .
your favorite cufflinks are sterling-silver replicas of water meter covers.

You know you're in New Orleans if . . .
you decide which shoes to wear to a funeral not by what best matches your outfit but by what would be most practical to parade in.

You know you're in New Orleans if . . .
you know there's a difference between Cajun and Creole, but you hope no one ever asks you because you can never remember exactly what that difference is.

You know you're in New Orleans if . . .
while mentioning to an acquaintance that you plan to drink burgundy on Burgundy, you don't pronounce any two words the same. Ditto for the calliope on Calliope.

Postscript: Crossing Blankets

After just a moment's hesitation, I walked across the ratty blue blanket spread out on the ground before me. It was just one in a long line of blankets and tarps stretched out like a patchwork snake on the neutral ground of St. Charles Avenue on Mardi Gras Day. After I had negotiated the headaches of parking and the throngs of people lining the route, this was my last obstacle. I was on the river side of St. Charles and the parade would be passing on the lake side. I had hesitated at the edge of the blanket because manners told me not to step on someone else's property, but then what right did these people have to claim public property and stop others from getting where they needed to go? The woman sitting on a folding chair in the middle of the blanket was surrounded by three young children. All three were huddled together against the cold. After making momentary eye contact with the woman, I walked right across her blanket.

"Could have asked first," I heard her say to herself but loudly enough for me to hear. I kept walking, congratulating myself for not turning around and giving her a piece of my mind. "You can't block people from crossing," I could have said. "You don't own this piece of property," I could have added. But I didn't.

Instead, I joined the rest of my family lining the parade route

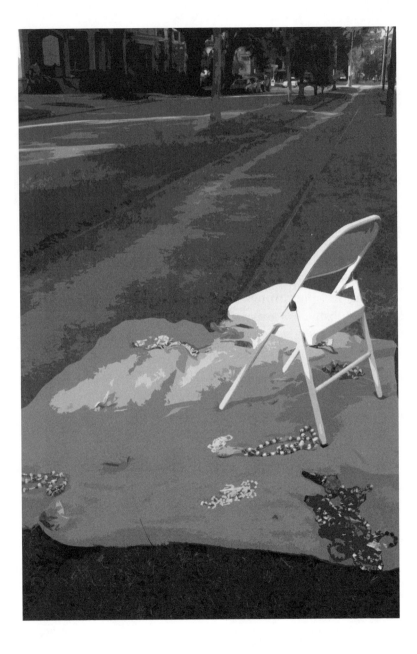

and fell in with the group, proud of myself for taking the moral high ground. The parade began. Floats and bands passed, but the blanket incident kept replaying in my head. I watched as people gave just-caught beads to strangers standing next to them; I saw a teen follow a rolling doubloon to the feet of an elderly lady sitting in a wheelchair behind a wall of ladders, pick up the doubloon, and then hand it to her.

It was a *"laissez les bons temps rouler"* atmosphere, and my indignation at the offending blanket seemed out of place. With a resigned sigh, I turned and walked back to the lady sitting in the chair on the blue blanket. When she realized who I was, her expression tightened.

"You're right," I said. "I could have asked first."

After studying me for a moment, she got up out of her chair and walked to the edge of the blanket, where I stood waiting for the tongue-lashing to come. "You're damned right you should have asked first," she could have said. "You had no right to walk across my blanket," she could have added. But she didn't. Instead, she gave me a big grin and put her arm around my shoulder.

"That's all I needed to hear, baby," she said. Then she pointed to the three children huddled on the blanket. "I'm sorry I got cross with you, but me and my children come to this same corner every year. I been here since five o'clock this morning trying to save this spot. That's why I gotta defend it—for the kids. But you can cross here anytime you want, baby. You're like family now."

I smiled. "Thanks."

Then she showed me a brown paper grocery bag next to her chair. "You let me know if you get hungry. We got some bologna sandwiches, Coke, and chips here. No ice for the Coke," she apologized, "but it's cold enough today you don't need no ice."

I politely declined. Inside the nearby apartment my family had rented for the parade season was a bounty of food so extensive it would take us another week to get through it: hot crawfish étouffée, roast beef po-boys, fried chicken, casseroles, kingcakes, hot coffee, and drinks. With ice. Compared to her fare, it seemed an embarrassment of riches. "No thanks. We brought some stuff with us," I explained.

"Okay, baby. If you need something later, let me know. I'll be back here. I don't like the commotion up front. We stay back here and we catch plenty enough."

I returned to my family on the parade route, feeling as if a burden had been lifted. Every once in a while I cast a glance back to make sure her kids were indeed catching enough. And they were.

After two hours of parades passing, one of the floats broke down, causing a long delay. She and her children huddled up under blankets. I made a point to get lost in the crowd first before entering the apartment for hot coffee, cozy warmth, and clean bathrooms. Without identification bracelets to show that she was among the families who had paid for the parade-season rental, she and her children would not be able to get past security, even at my invitation.

On my way back to the parade route, I brought a kingcake with me, hoping to sit on the blanket and share the cake with her and her children. But they were gone—their spot on St. Charles an empty square of crushed grass where the blanket had been. I found it strange that both of our families had apparently been sharing the same corner on St. Charles for years. Chances are that we had crossed paths sometime in the past, but we had never interacted, never bridged the gap between our two worlds.

Katrina hit six months later. My family has returned to our usual spot on St. Charles Avenue for subsequent Mardi Gras seasons, but the other family has not. If they weren't able to make it home, I'd like to think that at least they're happily resettled somewhere like Dallas or Chicago, rather than the awful alternative that they were among the grim statistics. Even so, there's no Mardi Gras in Dallas or Chicago.

Parade seasons will come and go, and I hope to be back on that corner, scrounging for beads and dancing to the marching bands. And I know that each time I'll cast a backward glance, hoping to see that family and their blue blanket on the St. Charles Avenue neutral ground. For this was their corner, too. And they should be here. Come hell or high water.